'Kirk Franklin introduces the challeng[...] God's Mission in the often-confusing g[...] standing of the issues at stake, coupled with keen historical and theological [...] Franklin not only encourages us to join the Triune God in his mission to the world, but also explains what it takes to be a missionary leader today. He knows what he is writing about— he has been in the field himself for decades. I highly recommend the book, not only for church leaders and missionary practitioners, but also for teachers and students in the field of missiology. It is a thought provoking publication that needs to be read carefully and discussed thoroughly by all.'

— **Piet Meiring**, Emeritus Professor of Missiology, University of Pretoria

'This is not a "standard" leadership book—it is a paradigm-changing leadership book. Kirk Franklin demonstrates that a new approach to global leadership is needed, one that displays generosity of spirit, values friendship among leaders, and invites missiological reflection in the context of community. These truths, and the others he introduces, are not only innovative and profound, but are modeled by Franklin himself, a leader whom we have seen authentically live these same values.'

— **Louis and Susan Sutton**, International Directors, WEC International

'Globalization has fundamentally transformed how missions function, including for those of us involved in the translation of Scriptures. Though much of this transformation has been positive, it has also raised questions. Kirk Franklin helps focus the discussion for us by stating the need for a "working theology of mission". In *Towards Global Missional Leadership*, Franklin provides the perspective and insight needed to start answering these questions.'

— **Bob Creson**, President/CEO, Wycliffe Bible Translators USA

'Kirk Franklin is not only a missiologist and missions practitioner, but also a well-proven leader in the global missional context. As Executive Director of the Wycliffe Global Alliance, he has successfully led great changes in organizational structure, as well as in strategy for this worldwide Bible translation community. The vision and philosophy behind the changes described in this book will help us see a new horizon of mission paradigm and leadership.'

— **Rev Dr Bambang Widjaja**, Board Chair, Indonesia People Network

'I am excited about Kirk Franklin's book *Towards Global Missional Leadership*. My journey in serving God over the past forty years has been an amazing learning experience, as I have walked alongside so many men and women from numerous countries and cultures, dedicated and committed to Jesus Christ. Meeting and spending time with Franklin has been a great joy, and I have observed him as he focused on the issues he speaks to in this book. It is an essential tool for the current and future mission leader.'

— **Decio de Carvalho**, Executive Director, COMIBAM Internacional

'A must read book for all involved in leading missions, whether global or local. Today's increasingly complex world brings challenges at a pace faster than we anticipate. Rather than counter this with new ideas about what to do, Franklin's book forces me to a stand-still—to reflect not only on *where* mission movements and endeavors have come from, but importantly, *why*. Before looking to the future, I must first reflect on my own relationship with the Triune God—a poignant reminder that it is God's mission, and only He can provide the answers! Read this book for refreshing insight into seeing and doing missions through the eyes and mind of God.'

— **Lena Lim**, Partner & Director, Browzwear Global

'To be a leader today is a challenge, as the global context is constantly changing. Many books are being produced to help us understand changing realities; only a handful are helping us understand how to lead in the middle of changing times. This is the first book I have read that challenged me to dig deeper into the *missio Dei* in order to understand leadership as a participant in God's mission. Kirk Franklin's book presents a unique per-spective that can help the church, global mission movements, and especially leaders, to gain a renewed appreciation of the missional DNA that God has shared with us.'

— **David D. Ruiz M.**, Executive Director, The Mission Commission,
World Evangelical Alliance

# TOWARDS GLOBAL
# MISSIONAL LEADERSHIP

*A Journey Through Leadership
Paradigm Shift in the Mission of God*

## KIRK J FRANKLIN

with Dave and Deborah Crough

FOREWORD

by Paul Bendor-Samuel

First published 2017 by Regnum Books International
in partnership with Wycliffe Global Alliance

Regnum is an imprint of the Oxford Centre for Mission Studies
St. Philip and St. James Church
Woodstock Road
Oxford, OX2 6HR, UK
www.ocms.ac.uk/regnum

Wycliffe Global Alliance: www.wycliffe.net

09 08 07 06 05 04 03 8 7 6 5 4 3 2 1

Design by Wes Franklin, Studio 164a

**British Library Cataloguing in Publication Data**
A catalogue record for this book is available from the British Library

ISBN: 978-1-506476-84-1

Distributed by 1517 Media in the US and Canada

# CONTENTS

**Foreword** by Paul Bendor-Samuel      7

**Preface**      11

**Introduction**      17

**Chapters**

1 The Triune God and the *Missio Dei*      21

2 Globalization and Glocalization in the *Missio Dei*      43

3 Paradigm Shifts and Polycentrism in the *Missio Dei*      61

4 Friendship and Community in the *Missio Dei*      77

5 Reflective Practitioners and the Consultative Process in the *Missio Dei*      91

6 Generosity in Spirit and Practice in the *Missio Dei*      105

7 Third Way Thinking in the *Missio Dei*      121

8 Forming a Global Missional Mindset      139

**Acknowledgements**      157

**Appendix:** Chapter Essay Contributors      159

**Notes**      163

**About the Author**      191

# FOREWORD

What, another book on leadership? Really? It's a fair question, particularly if, like me, you have read many books on leadership and have even more unread on your bookshelves already. Let me briefly describe three reasons why this book has enriched and challenged me.

First, it is authentic.

I have known Kirk Franklin for nearly a decade. We met through our experience of leading mature, international mission agencies in need of renewal. We have wrestled with similar challenges and looked for answers to the same questions. During this time I observed Kirk close up as he led the Wycliffe Global Alliance (WGA) on a journey of transformation. This journey has not been informed and shaped simply by the latest organizational management techniques, helpful as some of these may be. Rather, Kirk has envisioned and nurtured a journey shaped by missiological reflection: What does God's mission look like today, and how can we join him in it? This journey was not taken by a few senior leaders but by a 'mixed multitude' that has now increased to 100 organizations, from almost as many countries, and continues to grow.

Responding to challenges through the lens of missiological reflection has resulted in a total organizational transformation for WGA that is encouraging and influencing new Bible translation movements around the world and enabling the emergence of a new kind of leadership, the kind described in this book: global missional leadership. This book does not describe an elegant new theory of leadership dreamed up and designed in an academic laboratory. It describes the fruit of countless conversations, consultations and commitments to listening and learning in many different contexts. It's authentic.

Second, it's highly relevant.

One of the reasons for the multiplication of books on leadership is because excellence in leadership is so hard to deliver. Some years ago a number of international mission agencies recognised the need to become much more intentional about developing leaders and began to share ideas and resources. It quickly became apparent that all identified the need to develop a new kind of leader. This person would be capable of providing spiritual, missional and organizational leadership locally, while at the same time thinking and responding globally. None of us knew how to grow global leaders.

In recent months we have seen the overflow of powerful nationalistic forces in North America, the United Kingdom and Europe. These forces have been evident in other parts of the world for some years where religious and ethnic identity has become increasingly intertwined. In part this reflects a search for identity and meaning in the face of the apparently irresistible forces of globalization. Many feel the need to assert national, local identity over and against any sense of shared humanity. This is the context in which the Church is called to join God in his mission of reconciliation. There is an urgent need for the development of global missional leaders who are able to make sense of our times, and are capable of understanding and leading locally. It's relevant.

Third, it's reliable.

At the Oxford Centre for Mission Studies (OCMS), we enable over 125 scholar-practitioners from all over the world to engage in doctoral studies. A research PhD requires the use of primary sources of data. This data needs to be rigorously, critically and objectively analysed if a reliable thesis is to be developed. This book reflects the demanding work of collecting, analysing and interpreting real data. I believe that there is a reliable basis for Kirk's proposals for a new global missional leadership, something that we do well to pay attention to.

Finally, a word on why Regnum International is publishing this book in collaboration with WGA. Regnum is the publishing imprint of the OCMS. Over the years it has established itself as a dependable academic publisher. In 2017 we will complete the Edinburgh 2010 series, a set of 35 volumes of mission studies with over 600 contributors from around the world, representing the best of scholarship from all the major streams of Christian spirituality.

While we delight to serve the academic community, our mission is to enable the global church to better engage in God's mission in its very diverse contexts. To do this we seek to bring practitioners and academics together. This book launches a new Regnum Practitioner series. Our desire is that this series will bridge the gap that sometimes exists between, on the one hand, Christian leaders and mission practitioners and, on the other, Christian researchers. Where better to start than with a fresh look at what is required of leadership in mission and the church?

Dr Paul Bendor-Samuel MBE, MRCGP
Executive Director, Oxford Centre for Mission Studies
January 2017

# PREFACE

In 2007, while visiting him at his home in Pretoria, South Africa, Prof Piet Meiring offered to be my promoter and for me to study under him for a PhD at the Department of Science of Religion and Missiology, Faculty of Theology, University of Pretoria. However, I ended up needing to prove to the University that I could handle the rigors of research by completing a BA (Honours) in 2009. By the time I was ready for an MA, Prof Meiring had retired. But he introduced me to Prof Nelus Niemandt who became my promoter. During 2010-12, I researched this topic for my MA: 'The Wycliffe Global Alliance: From a U.S. Based International Mission to a Global Movement for Bible Translation'.

When I finished, I thought that was it. I'd had enough of academic life and work. A PhD was not going to happen. I even told this to my friend and colleague, Dr Stephen Coertze, as he accompanied me to hand in my MA thesis. However, Prof Niemandt encouraged me to take one 'slice' of the thesis and expand it through a PhD under him. By the end of 2012, the university's research and ethics committees had approved my research plan, with the topic: 'A Paradigm for Global Mission Leadership: The Journey of the Wycliffe Global Alliance'. I started in late 2012, made little progress in 2013 and early 2014, then devised and began an intensive writing phase in May-August 2015. The internal and external examination took place in November-December 2015. The final work was successfully orally defended in February 2016.

One of my external examiners wrote in his report:

> It has been a pleasure to read this thesis, which... engaged across a number of significant intersecting themes important for God's mission in our globalised world today.... I believe it is a helpful piece of research [with] many insights and conclusions which would be helpful, not only for other mission agencies, but also for those leading churches, which are... facing the same challenges and influenced by the same forces.... It is excellent to see a piece

of work that not only provides helpful insights on the kinds of changes needed today, but also grounds them in solid research and provides some insights into a helpful process of change.

These words enthused me to give serious thought to making the research more widely available. This was followed by feedback from international mission leaders who heard me speak on themes associated with the research, and encouraged me to produce a book that would hold the attention of busy leaders in Christian ministry, whether church, mission agencies or other spheres of service and influence. I took their recommendation seriously, and with the help of colleagues Dave and Deborah Crough, this book has come to fruition.

It was not my personal ambition or goal to write such a book, especially one that has academic research as its foundation. My journey in academia has not been a smooth one.

In 1977, after only a year of Bible college and a semester at a US liberal arts college, I dropped out of school. I had not talked this over first with my parents, even though I was living at home at the time. This was devastating news to them. They may have thought that I would not have any direction in life, and that was true for the time being. School had always been a struggle for me, and this was not helped by dyslexia that was undetected until much later.

That same year, despite my protests, my mother intervened in my aimless life and got me a job interview at a local printing company. I got the job and discovered I could excel at printing, then graphic arts, then later, photography and graphic design. All of these fields are primarily visual. I joined Wycliffe Bible Translators with those skills and went back to the place of my birth, Papua New Guinea (PNG). That is how Christine and I met, as she was a schoolteacher there. In 1987, while serving in PNG, I took two subjects at MA level in leadership by extension from Azusa Pacific University. I earned the best academic results I had ever made. I was motivated, as I was now in a leadership role and I wanted to lead well.

I did not attempt any further study and the two subjects didn't count towards an MA since I didn't have the prerequisite BA. By 2000 I was serving as the Executive Director of Wycliffe Australia when one of my

Board members encouraged me to meet with Dr Les Henson, a missiologist at Tabor College Victoria. I enrolled in a BA in Intercultural Studies under him. I was dedicated and did well, and graduated in 2004.

When I started as the Executive Director for the Wycliffe Global Alliance in 2008, I asked my Board for their approval to do post-graduate studies. The condition the chairman, Rev Roger Welch, set was that I needed to study at an institution in the global South and East. He wanted my mind to be stimulated by leaders and theologians from other parts of the world than where I was from or familiar with. This was sound advice and I thoroughly enjoyed studying in South Africa.

A reoccurring theme during the last eight years of research and writing has been the Apostle Paul's words where he admits that despite the extraordinarily powerful message he proclaims, he does so as a vulnerable human being: 'We carry this precious Message around in the unadorned clay pots of our ordinary lives. That's to prevent anyone from confusing God's incomparable power with us' (2 Corinthians 4:7 MSG).

The Old Testament uses the imagery of jars of clay as a metaphor for human weakness: 'Remember that you have made me as with the clay; will you return me to dust?' (Job 10:9 NET). Or 'Yet, Lord, you are our father. We are the clay, and you are our potter; we are all the product of your labor' (Isaiah 64:8 NET). The contrast between the fragile container and its precious contents has a purpose. It is to show that this all surpassing power is from God and not from us.

In this account that I have shared with you, you may note a theme of personal weakness and vulnerability. I never set out to swim in the deep waters of the research world, let alone think I could make a contribution to the field of theology and leadership in global mission. God through his divine will has taken me from being a photographer-graphic designer without formal training, to now a completed PhD, from which studies this book is based. With that I declare: To God be the glory!

Back to the book itself —through the eight chapters, short essays and study questions, I hope that you will gain insights by way of perhaps otherwise unconnected thoughts about leadership in the global context, and especially leadership in global ministry.

This book is not intended to be exhaustive in covering all there is to know about any single topic. Instead, the interplay of the topics is the key to consider how to frame and lead in a new paradigm.

Certain contents of the book will soon appear, or have appeared in publication before, and I am grateful to the editors and publishers for the works involved as noted here.

The chief resource for the book is content drawn from the PhD thesis, 'A Paradigm for Global Mission Leadership: The Journey of the Wycliffe Global Alliance' by Kirk Franklin, University of Pretoria, South Africa, 2016, with some additional material drawn from the MA thesis, 'The Wycliffe Global Alliance: From a U.S. Based International Mission to a Global Movement for Bible Translation' by Kirk Franklin, University of Pretoria, South Africa, 2012.

Some content from Chapter 6 appeared in the article, 'Funding God's Mission' by Kirk Franklin and C.J.P. (Nelus) Niemandt in *Missionalia* 43(3), 384-409, 2015, and used with permission. Some content from Chapter 3 appeared in the article, 'Polycentrism in the *Missio Dei*' by Kirk Franklin and C.J.P. (Nelus) Niemandt in *HTS Teologiese Studies/Theological Studies* 72(1), 2016, (http://dx.doi.org/10.4102/hts.v72i1.3145). Though this is an open source publication, acknowledgement is nonetheless given to the publishers. Acknowledgement and appreciation is given to Prof Nelus Niemandt as co-author of both of these articles and for his permission to use the material.

Some of the content in Chapters 1 and 8 appears in similar form in 'Mission and Spirituality' by Kirk Franklin, in Taylor, W., Hahn, G., and Amaraj, J. (eds.), *Spirituality and Mission*, a forthcoming publication in 2017, and used with permission. Finally, portions of content in Chapters 5 and 8 appear in 'A Model for Leadership Communities in Global Contexts' by Kirk Franklin in Barentsen, Jack, Steven C. van den Heuvel, and Peirong Lin, eds., *The End of Leadership? Leadership and Authority at Crossroads*, Vol. 4, Christian Perspectives on Leadership and Social Ethics. Leuven: Peeters, 2017, pages 83-106, and used by permission of Peeters Publishers.

# INTRODUCTION

**W**hy this book with quite a long title: 'Towards Global Missional Leadership: A Journey Through Leadership Paradigm Shift in the Mission of God'? My purpose in writing this book is to bring increased awareness to the developing concept-to-reality of global missional leadership, and leadership-in-community. These two perspectives compliment each other and help us lead not just in some form of global mission but also in any context where organizations, church and agencies are engaged in some form of global ministry.

I must emphasize, however, that since this new paradigm is evolving, if you currently lead in an institutional model, you can still seek to bring change within your organization even if is not global in scope. In other words, being a leader in some form of global ministry is not essential in order to begin developing a global missional mindset. Many of the principles can apply more broadly. Effects of the changing global context still greatly impact one's local context, including one's churches and other agencies. For example, the benefits of creating third spaces, or leading from the context of generosity, or practicing reflectivity in leading still apply in local situations.

This is the challenge I raise up front: if the concept is new or unfamiliar don't cast it aside. Explore it more fully through what is presented here and then make some small steps to put it into practice. We become leaders with a global mindset not through one big leap but through hundreds of smaller steps.

There is terminology used throughout the book that needs to be explained. First of all, it is problematic to make geographical statements about the growth or location of the church worldwide. For instance, when referring to the 'Western church' or the 'West' in general it is more appropriate in Latin America to refer to the West as the 'North' since the US and Canada are located in the North, not the West. Another problematic term is the 'global South' or the 'church of the southern continents' (e.g. Africa, Asia, the Pacific Islands, the Caribbean and Latin America). A more accurate description is to add 'East' since the church in Korea and China are in the East, not the South. Therefore, for the sake of continuity in this book, when the terms 'West' or 'Western' are used, they include those who prefer 'North' or 'Northern' terminology. Likewise, 'global South and East' is used instead of other variants.

Secondly, in the context of mission agencies, there is a significant distinction between the terms 'international' and 'global'. The word 'international' is semantically tied to a Western concept of territorial expansion. Furthermore, many mission agencies use 'international' in their name, but the location of their headquarters and the nationalities of their leadership teams and/or governing bodies indicate they are still Western based and controlled. The 21st century church has spread globally, and mission structures may still be catching up with the consequences. Therefore, as mission agencies understand the changing dynamics of the church, the term global is a preferred term to international.

Lastly, an abbreviation is used in numerous instances throughout the book—WGA, which stands for the Wycliffe Global Alliance.

In order to prepare you as you delve into the content ahead, here are seven factors affecting and influencing the early stages of the paradigm shift that is underway that are explored in the forthcoming chapters:

1. Global mission contexts require missional leaders-in-community who are equipped to lead change, as well as to learn from and respond to far greater cultural diversity than previous generations of mission leaders.

2. Also needed are global missional leaders who can provide change in discontinuous contexts, which is the new norm. Their predecessors were more familiar with leading in an atmosphere of continuous change. According to Alan Roxburgh and Fred Romanuk, continuous change is when situations are more or less predictable and the process of change becomes an outcome of what has gone before, and it can be anticipated and managed. In contrast, discontinuous change disrupts the status quo, challenges existing assumptions, creates a

tipping point to something new, and therefore requires an unlearning of what was known before so that a new contextual mindset can be developed.[1]

3. There is less demarcation between high-context and low-context cultures due to globalization. Robert Vecchio notes that high-context cultures value the group and cooperation, harmonious relationships and a heightened awareness of their physical settings. Low-context cultures prefer individualism, competition and explicit communication and ideas.[2] Nonetheless, global missional leaders must learn cultural intelligence in order to navigate in a globalized world.

4. Developing trust provides a foundation based upon justice and love within and between diverse missional communities. This needs greater priority since more people from more cultures are participating in God's mission. John Crossan cautions that if justice and love are separated from each other, there will be 'brutality [or] banality'.[3]

5. Missional structures need to be developed that enable leaders from the global South and East to influence global mission strategy.

6. Positive missional role models are needed, especially in situations more familiar with hierarchical leadership models. This includes models that encourage followers to raise questions and to think creatively and interdependently.

7. Models are needed that appreciate and support courageous missional leadership, providing change that builds consensus in complex cross-cultural, multi-cultural and inter-cultural contexts.

As you begin the journey of this book, note that each chapter has discussion questions that can be used for personal reflection, or especially for conversation and exchange of views in small groups. Each chapter can be held on its own, for study and dialogue on the various topics presented.

You will find a sidebar within each chapter except the concluding one. These are short essays written by leaders whom I know and approached because of their own experiences that are relevant to the topic being covered. Their insights enrich the book.

Now it is time to get going on your global missional leadership journey and the paradigm shifts that lie ahead.

# The Triune God and the *Missio Dei*

I was wide-awake in the middle of a hot summer night in Melbourne in February 1997. Unable to sleep, the Lord prompted me to get out of bed and start writing. Zechariah 4:6 kept coming to mind: 'This is the word of the LORD to Zerubbabel: "Not by might nor by power, but by my Spirit," says the LORD Almighty.' I wrote it down and started studying the passage and the events surrounding it. Zerubbabel was the leader of Jewish exiles (Haggai 1:2-9), and God rebuked them for losing sight of their mandate to rebuild God's temple. They had become sidetracked, interrupted by opposition and focusing on their own interests, such as building nice houses for themselves. Then the Word of God came to Zerubbabel: the task could not be accomplished in his own strength, yet in the Lord's strength, 'nothing, not even a mighty mountain, will stand in Zerubbabel's way; it will become a level plain before him!' (Zechariah 4:7 NLT).

This event had a profound effect, like a lightning bolt flashing in my face and completely stunning me. I realized I was behaving like Zerubbabel and the exiles, easily distracted, and prone to operate in my own limited strength. Excited by this revelation from God's word, I shared the experience with the media department of Wycliffe Australia, the team I was working with at the time. We decided to mount Zechariah 4:6 on our meeting room wall so we would be daily reminded of God's word prompting us to rely upon him.

Almost a year to the day after that restless night, I was appointed by the Board of Wycliffe Australia to be Executive Director for that organization. As I took up the leadership role, I kept the words of Zechariah 4:6 firmly in my mind.

Today I am leading the Wycliffe Global Alliance (WGA) in rapidly changing, complex social, cultural, economic, political and religious contexts. Each presents unique challenges and obstacles. It is a natural tendency to think I can accumulate the skills and experience to master any leadership problems or complexities in front of me. The reality of being a leader in God's mission means spending significant energy on developing plans, strategies, budgets, and of course, outcomes. Mission history is known for having men and women who believed they had the vision and faith to achieve outcomes for God's mission. My experience, however, is that leaders easily miss out on digging deeper into understanding God and his ways and means for mission through our relentless activity. We lead in mission without an awareness of the significance of the *missio Dei*—God's mission.

This should be an alarming concern: Christian mission is actually very vulnerable. Scottish church historian Andrew Walls notes how some world religions have maintained allegiance across the centuries, but not so with the Christian faith. Do we remember that Yemen was once a Christian kingdom, Syria had a church influence that led the Christian world, and Christianity was strong in the whole Euphrates valley (modern Iraq)? Walls therefore concludes, 'Christian advance is not steady inevitable progress. Advance is often followed by recession.' The spread of the gospel does not conquer and hold new territory because at the very heart of the gospel is the 'vulnerability of the Cross and the fragility of the earthen vessel'.[1] As the Apostle Paul states, 'we have this treasure in clay jars, so that the extraordinary power belongs to God and does not come from us' (2 Corinthians 4:7 NET).

## God in Three Persons Asks for an RSVP

Why begin a book about leadership-in-community with the Holy Trinity?

While an answer is more than hinted at in the question, the real reason is about the element of mystery. Though they are revealed to us in Scripture, there is an undeniable component of something beyond human understanding regarding God the Father, God the Son and God the Holy Spirit.

To a great extent, our triune God remains a mystery to us.

Through this book's pages, as we survey the changing global contexts impacting so much of how we think of ourselves and our church's or agency's roles in the world, we can lay hold of this eternal truth as a bedrock foundation: that God has not only proclaimed his redemptive nature, but invited us to join in his ultimate desire for complete restoration of the world and all that is in it.

That God's people are invited to join in this is a further mystery.

This gives rise to a basic premise presented throughout this book—there is no formula or new methodology, there are no defined next steps showing those in leadership how to cope with increasingly interconnected global issues. Instead, the best place to start, and a key purpose of this book, is to gain missiological-based understanding of not only whom we serve, but within what overarching context: The Triune God and the *Missio Dei*.

To begin discussing the Trinity in relation to mission as foundational understanding for the rest of this book, let's look at writings from the not-too-distant past. In the 1990's, noted theologian and missiologist Lesslie Newbigin's Trinitarian emphasis of mission gained influence. Newbigin stated that God is ruler over all and therefore the church boldly proclaims the kingdom of God as being 'over all things'.[2] The triune God is where the church's understanding of mission should start.[3] The church 'acts out the love of Jesus that took him to the cross' when it invites people into a union with Jesus Christ, who in this world is 'the presence of the kingdom'. The Holy Spirit as the 'preview' of God's kingdom directs the church into the world, often in mysterious ways.[4]

There's that notion of 'mystery' again. Not in reference to the nature or authority of God, but rather in how the church acts under God's direction. According to Newbigin, mission involves all members of the triune God: the Father proclaims the kingdom, the Son offers new life, and the Holy Spirit bears witness to the activity of the triune God.[5] Timothy Tennent states it is only through the triune God that the church has 'missional authority' to proclaim and demonstrate the gospel. The issue of authority is important. Under Christendom's influence, biblical

Trinitarian authority for mission was 'replaced by a cultural, institutional, or pragmatic one'. [6]

Historically, the meaning of 'Christendom' was about identity at a society-wide level. It was not based upon a personal faith in Christ, but was a consequence of belonging to a particular Christian denomination or nation. David Bosch notes that effects of a thousand years of Christendom are how the Western form of Christianity has lost its predominant place in global Christianity.[7] Jonathan Bonk suggests that Christendom's self-confidence peaked in the post-1910 era. [8]

Since the Christendom term is still used, a number of meanings are common: (1) Western European Christianity, commencing with Roman emperor Constantine's incredible support of the church with special imperial favours and status; (2) a description of anyplace where 'Christian forms and structures are firmly entrenched within a society';[9] and (3) Philip Jenkins' description of the spread of Christianity to the majority world as the new or 'next' Christendom that is the global church.[10]

Of prominence for our purposes here is the observation that over time, man-made constructs, often in the form of institutional mandates, influenced and eroded the biblical Trinitarian basis for mission. Thus, the call for a Trinitarian missiology by Newbigin is a call to *return* to the authority of the triune God in mission.

*That* is key for leadership to grasp and instil as foundational understanding among colleagues and partners, no matter what the focus of ministry is.

Further, in terms of the church and mission across the world, Tennent postulates a Trinitarian mission that is 'simultaneously God centred and church focused' as God graciously invites the church to join him in his mission.[11] The triune God gives the church its role in his mission.[12] This is 'the whole church taking the whole gospel to the whole person in the whole world'.[13] In other words, this is the complete responsibility God has given the church 'for the salvation of the world'.[14] The scope of God's mission is to 'restore all nations [and] all cultures from the sinful rebellion of humankind and its effects'.[15]

As mission is primarily about God and his 'redemptive purposes and initiatives in the world', then the gospel of Jesus Christ is the heart of the mission of the Trinitarian God.[16] In relation to this truth, mission is also interested in the actions, tasks, strategies and initiatives that the church may assume.[17]

Ultimately, mission is 'God's redemptive, historical initiative on behalf of His creation'. Meanwhile, *missions* is all of the various and specific ways that 'the church crosses cultural boundaries'[18] in order to give 'witness to the reality of God through the church as the sign, foretaste and presence of the kingdom'.[19]

But we're getting a little ahead of ourselves, and will come back to more discussion about mission in the next section. In terms of the source of mission, Bosch stated that mission originates only from the heart of the triune God who acts as a 'fountain of sending love'.[20] This is the 'deepest source of mission'.[21] The meaning of mission is found in the

## The Triune God in Mission

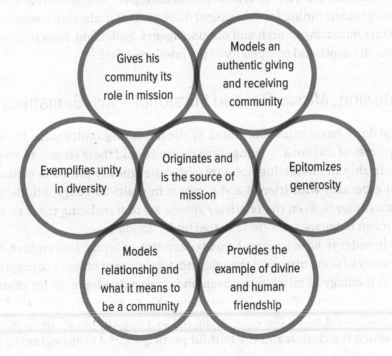

Gives his community its role in mission

Models an authentic giving and receiving community

Exemplifies unity in diversity

Originates and is the source of mission

Epitomizes generosity

Models relationship and what it means to be a community

Provides the example of divine and human friendship

relationship within the Trinity expressed in this progression: the Father sends the Son, the Father and the Son send the Holy Spirit. The Father, Son and Holy Spirit send the church into the world.[22] The end result of God's mission will be a state of *shalom* when God's 'universal reconciliation and peace' will reign over all.[23]

Theologian Georg Vicedom wanted greater clarity to the relationship of mission to the Trinity by observing that the triune God is the model for influencing mission's spirit and action.[24] It is the loving will and nature of God that provides the origin and basis for mission and the church as the instrument for mission.[25] The ownership of mission is entirely with God from start to finish.[26]

The activity of the individual Christian in God's mission is part of a larger community, modelled by the members of the community of the triune God, in which each has 'individual identity and tasks [that] are unified in the corporate identity and purpose of the godhead'.[27]

This brief overview of Trinitarian missiological thought forms a necessary underpinning for subsequent discussion of leadership issues, and factors impacting church and mission agency leadership. Now let's consider the depth and complexity of the mission of God.

## Mission, *Missio Dei* and Missional—Just Semantics?

And don't forget missions, plural. While not taking centre stage for the purposes of this book, gaining some clarity around these terms can assist leadership in interacting not only with colleagues of the same culture, but especially with friends and partners in multi-language, multi-cultural contexts. Even the relatively simple act of translating these terms in major languages can erode shared understanding.

In order to have a common understanding of terms, let's embark on a survey of some historical thought and development of these concepts.

A theology of mission has been undergoing development for centuries. For example, Thomas Kemper notes that St Augustine (354-430 CE) is credited for using the term *missio Dei* as a description of 'God's work in which the church and the faithful participate'.[28] At the beginning of the Protestant Reformation, Martin Luther's (1483-1546 CE) views of the work of God and the arrival of God's kingdom could be described as an emerging theology of mission. In the 16th century, Gisbertus Voetius stated that mission flowed from the heart of God. Much later, Bosch observed how up to the 16th century, the concept of *missio Dei* was associated with the doctrine of the Trinity.[29] Kemper suggests that it was really only from 1952 onwards that the concept of the mission of God was articulated in a more far-reaching manner.[30]

With this in mind, the intent of this section is to consider the theological developments surrounding mission, *missio Dei*, and missional—and for our purposes, we'll begin in the 1800's.

## Mission as Western conquest and persuasion

Walls observes two simultaneous approaches to mission that contributed to the expansion of the Christian faith in the 19th century. The first is the 'crusading mode' when some missionaries aligned with colonial Christendom governments and compared God's mission to a military conquest, with a concomitant expansion of territory. Christianity was thought to be superior and would Christianize entire people groups. Western education was one vehicle (whether in English or the local vernacular) for expansion.[31] The second approach is 'the missionary mode', where Christian missionaries sought to sincerely and truthfully proclaim the gospel and seek out new followers to disciple in their faith.

At the Edinburgh World Missionary Conference of 1910, Robert Speer promoted mission as 'conquest'.[32] At the close of the conference, chairman John Mott boldly proclaimed that a conquest to the ends of the earth by world mission had begun. He logically believed that all available Christian resources would be quickly deployed to support this advance.[33] Those present in the conference would be responsible for initiating a comprehensive plan for evangelization that would see the world completely 'reached' in the foreseeable future.[34]

This Edinburgh optimism was disrupted by the onslaught of World War I (1914-1918), the Great Depression (1929-1933) and World War II

(1939-1945). These cataclysmic events challenged optimistic mission rhetoric because

- The collapse of the European empires meant a significant loss of influence of colonialism.
- The over-confidence arising from the Enlightenment was ill-founded—presuming that humanity could 'change the world'.[35]
- Western Christian leaders realized that the church was growing more rapidly outside of the West than it was in Europe.
- A humbler approach to mission was characterized as the realization of the depravity of the sinful human condition and its separation from God.[36]

## Tensions in mission theology

A series of gatherings of the International Mission Council (IMC) sought to pick up where Edinburgh left off. (The IMC later integrated into the World Council of Churches.) Starting in Jerusalem (1928), differences of opinion arose between those who thought mission was evangelism through proclamation, and those who saw mission as focused on the social implications of the gospel.[37]

At the Tambaram, India IMC conference (1938), further conflicts developed. William Ernest Hocking questioned the lack of cooperation with followers of other religions, whom he saw as allies against the mutual foe of secularism. Hendrick Kramer, on the other hand, emphasized mission as primarily the proclamation of the gospel.

At the Whitby, Canada IMC conference (1947), the post World War II mood was one of submitting to God as his humble partners in mission.

Earlier, at the 1932 Brandenburg IMC conference, Karl Barth introduced Protestant reflections on the characterization of mission in his paper, 'Theology and Mission'. Barth's conceptualization of mission is the 'activity of God'. Mission is 'a witness' to the action and activity of God himself on behalf of the world and for all humanity.[38] Mission is therefore fully dependent upon Christ's grace. It is an action arising from the heart of the triune God.[39] The key point: Barth moved the ownership of mission from the church to God.

Barth's contemporaries did not view him as a 'friend' of mission. However, his Trinitarian emphasis has influenced a wider circle of theological development on where mission was centred: it originated as God's activity rather than the human activity of the church.[40]

## *Missio Dei's* theological development

At the Willingen, Germany IMC (1952), Karl Hartenstein built upon Barth's Trinitarian emphasis of mission. At Willingen, Hartenstein popularized the term *missio Dei* for the first time and positioned mission 'as the cause of the Trinitarian God', rather than as the obligation of the church.[41] Hartenstein stated that mission occurred within the triune God's overall plan for salvation because 'God is mission'.[42] Kemper also observes that Barth's influence meant mission was the labour of the triune God as an absolute 'missionary God [because] mission is an attribute of God'.[43, 44]

Such considerations continued the profound shift that had started with Barth. Rather than mission originating from the church, or being church-centred,[45] the triune God initiates mission and empowers the church to go into the whole world.[46] Francis Anekwe Oborji states that 'the church exists because there is *missio Dei*'.[47] However, the church's role is not marginalized in mission, even though God's mission is greater than the missionary actions of the church itself.[48] The church's role is to be 'an instrument of mission... in the movement of God's love' for all of humanity.[49]

After the Willingen IMC, *missio Dei* was mentioned but not given widespread use until 1958 when Vicedom used the term in his book *The Mission of God* (in German, with an English translation in 1964). The Latin phrase *missio Dei* literally means, 'the sending of God' or 'the mission of God'.

The IMC in Mexico City (1963) brought together mission and evangelism that had previously been separated. Mission was no longer a one-directional action from the 'West to the rest' but was occurring in all directions.[50] Mission was no longer limited to the church's activity of sending cross-cultural missionaries overseas, and no longer based primarily on geography. Instead, mission was founded upon the 'belief, conviction and commitment' of all that the church was sent to do, starting first with where it was found.[51]

## *Missio Dei's* widening influence

J.C. Hoekendijk understood *missio Dei* as based upon 'God's self-revelation as the One who loves the world'.[52] God's action is in and with the world, and he invites the church to participate with him in the world in specific methods, 'times and places, or in response to particular needs'.[53] God also continues to care for his creation and bring *shalom* to the earth because the 'world sets the agenda for the church'.[54]

While Hoekendijk's position gained popularity, others saw the church's role in the *missio Dei* as the principal channel by which God's redemption occurs in the world.[55]

The San Antonio (1989) Conference on World Mission and Evangelism resulted in a broader acceptance of *missio Dei* by wider spheres of the church, including evangelicals, mainline Protestants, Eastern Orthodox and Roman Catholics. Mission was now considered to be 'multi-dimensional' as it responded to a growing agenda into every context imaginable.[56]

## *Missio Dei* and David Bosch

Bosch's work on refining the understanding of *missio Dei* cannot be underestimated. His *Transforming Mission* continues to be extensively cited on the topic. Bosch observed how God's mission had been interpreted through mission history in a number of ways:

- In soteriological terms 'as saving individuals from eternal damnation'.
- In cultural terms as bringing the so called 'blessings of the Christian West' to people from the global South and East.
- In ecclesiastical terms as the physical growth of the church or a denomination.

- In salvation history as the manner that the world becomes 'transformed into the kingdom of God'.[57]

## Influence of the Lausanne Movement

The Lausanne Committee for World Evangelization (LCWE)—later the Lausanne Movement—released its *Covenant* in 1974. This has influenced evangelical understanding of mission because it states that, within the church's mission, 'evangelism is primary' (LCWEa).[58] Later, Lausanne's *Manila Manifesto* (1979) states that mission encompasses the 'whole gospel' that establishes the kingdom of God on earth through his 'liberating plan' for his redeemed community (LCWEb).[59]

This is an important shift since many mission societies founded in the 19th century were motivated by a priority on evangelism that emphasized the penal substitutionary theory of the atonement.[60]

In the Lausanne Movement's *Cape Town Commitment* (2010), it states that the redemption of all of creation through Jesus Christ is the focus of the establishment of God's kingdom, which seeks to transform all nations. Therefore, mission is the integration of evangelism and the demonstration (or 'committed engagement') of the gospel in the world. Proclamation has social outcomes when people are called to 'love and repentance', and social participation has evangelistic implications when the church bears witness to Christ's 'transforming grace'. Since God has a redemptive plan for all of creation, the *Commitment* urges Christians to critical and 'prophetic ecological responsibility' because of the wastage of the earth's resources and corresponding rampant consumerism.[61]

Christopher Wright brings clarity to a definition of mission by anchoring it in a missiological hermeneutic of the Bible: Mission is the 'committed participation of God's people in the purposes of God for the redemption of the whole creation'. Then, almost in wonderment at this pronouncement, Wright states that God invites people to join with him because he chooses to uses fragile human instruments in his mission through our involvement in planning and in our action.[62]

## Shifts in understanding mission

Daryl Balia and Kirsteen Kim reflect on the centenary of the Edinburgh 1910 World Missionary Conference and provide contrasts that took place in 100 years of development of a theology of mission: In 1910, the focus was on the *'missions* of the churches [or] church-centred mission'. By 2010 this has shifted to God's mission (*missio Dei*) in which Christians participate (or a 'mission-centred church') and are looking for 'missionary collaboration beyond the church'. In 1910 there was the understanding of multiplicity of missions; 100 years later, while mission is referred to in the singular sense, it is multifaceted because it includes 'witness, proclamation, catechesis, worship, inculturation [and] interfaith dialogue', all carried out in specific situations. Understanding God's mission has moved from 'ecclesiology and soteriology' to a Trinitarian perspective as the foundation.[63]

Another type of shift is from mission originating from well-established and resourced centres towards 'the margins' of the less affluent parts of the world.[64] Those at the margins are the new agents of mission who state that mission is 'transformation'.[65]

## 21st century shifts in interpreting mission

Laying a foundation for mission in the 21st century, Cathy Ross identifies five indicators of mission that are intentionally broad and inclusive:

1. pronouncing the good news of God's kingdom;
2. teaching, baptising and nurturing new believers;
3. responding to human needs by loving acts of service;
4. finding ways to change 'unjust structures of society'; and
5. attempting to uphold the 'integrity of creation' and care for it.[66]

Kim goes further and notes two transitions in understanding mission: (1) it is no longer the sole domain and responsibility of cross-cultural missionaries who are sent to distant, un-evangelized lands. Instead, mission is fundamental to being the church, and to being God's people in the church; and (2) it is no longer a group of tasks expected by God to be carried out by Christians. Instead, it is the 'spontaneous outwork-ing' of the Holy Spirit who inspires Christians to participate in God's 'life-giving work'.[67]

Other related shifts include

- the 'content' of mission changing from being solely about evangelism to a comprehensive focus of proclamation and demonstration of the gospel;
- the 'means' of mission shifting from well-equipped specialist mission agencies to multifaceted partnerships in mission, regardless of how well-resourced they are;
- the 'context' for mission transitioning from 'the West to the rest' to 'everyone/everywhere-to-everywhere'; and
- the 'attitude' in mission moving from its Western-Enlighten-ment-Christendom outlook to dealing with complex influences from post-modernism, the impact of globalization and world religions.[68]

### Holistic emphasis

Understanding of God's mission has gained in both maturity and depth. God gives the church his mandate to join him in his love for and care of the world. The aim of mission, therefore, is to establish Christ as Lord over *all* of his creation. The Bible, theology and the experiences of God's people are the means that God uses to accomplish this purpose.[69]

Simangaliso Kumalo, writing from an African perspective, defines mission to include God's work of redemption *and* liberation, so that both individuals and society experience 'lasting transformation'. In this sense mission is comprehensive, incorporating all of the multifaceted activities of God's faith community by bringing God's fullness to all of humankind. Kumalo emphasizes the human contribution to mission by stating that without people participating, the *missio Dei* is at best 'ideal-istic'.[70] Latin American Néstor Miguez sees mission as calling the church to build the community of faith and be actively involved in the care of creation, as part of the agenda of God, the creator.[71]

These visions of mission are what John Driver calls holistic, because they are based upon God's plan for justice and *shalom*.[72] God's agenda of *missio Dei* for his kingdom contributes to wholeness in the church's involvement in his mission. This holistic emphasis keeps the church from being preoccupied about its own self-preservation.

## Interpreting *missio Dei*

Interpreting the *missio Dei* through theological grids is an on-going and challenging proposition due to its diverse interpretation and application. Consequently, Gary Tyra refers to the *missio Dei* as an 'elastic concept' that continuously integrates new meanings.[73] While God's actions are wide-ranging, there are aspects that do not change such as 'his relational, self-giving, grace-filled nature'.[74]

John Flett notes that despite fifty years of theological reflection on the *missio Dei*, there still is a 'lack of cohesion' and coordination concerning the three elements that he states make up the *missio Dei*:

1.  its Trinitarian basis,
2.  its orientation towards the kingdom of God, and
3.  its human instrumentality—the 'missionary nature of the church'. Such is this challenge that Flett refers to it as 'a bog of elasticity' because, despite its Trinitarian basis, *missio Dei* always has 'anthropological grounding'.[75]

The expanding theological discussion about mission is dynamic. On the one hand, Bosch states that mission should not be defined too narrowly because it is 'multidimensional' and covers a broad spectrum, including 'witness, service, justice, healing, reconciliation, liberation, peace, evangelism, fellowship, church planting, contextualization, and much more'.[76] On the other hand, Stephen Neill warns, 'if everything is mission, then nothing is mission'.[77] Likewise, J. Andrew Kirk states that if defining mission goes unconstrained it could lose its significance and be taken for granted, or perhaps serve as a theme for simplistic mission catchphrases.[78]

## Missional

Missional is an adjective describing the qualities and attributes of something related to mission and/or characterized by the mission of God.[79] This can be applied to a church or organizational structure, a mission objective, a title, an activity, and so forth.[80]

The book *Missional Church: A Vision for the Sending of the Church in North America* edited by Darrell Guder[81] brought the term into mainstream use, and it quickly began appearing in theological and missiological works in the early 21st century. According to Lois Barrett even the title of this book was done deliberately and evocatively to signify that a new paradigm was underway.[82] It was shifting the use of the word missionary to missional because missionary implied the cross-cultural factor rather than recognizing everything the church does is missional.

Charles Van Engen makes overt use of 'missional' in his 1991 work, *God's Missionary People*. His use of missional is 'an adjective describing relationships' of those involved in mission.[83] For example, Van Engen provides evidence that the church is missional when it participates in the triune God's transformation of the world.[84]

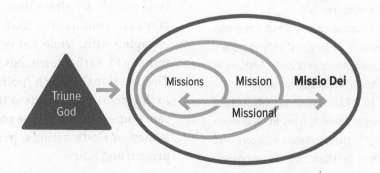

**The Missional Context:** "Missional" describes such things as relationships, purpose and identity of churches and organizations— and their leadership—within the *missio Dei*. The term characterizes both activities and intent along a spectrum in the context of God's mission.

# The Mission of God is not the Messenger of God

## by Stephen Coertze

t is said that by the 16th century, every ship sailing from Europe to the new world was loaded with soldiers and administrators whose duty it was to conquer and manage new territories. Also on board were Christian missionaries who would fulfill the purposes of both the Church and State. This alignment with colonial Christendom governments made it difficult for the recipients of mission to discern the difference between the coming of the colonial powers and the coming of the kingdom of God.

My home country, South Africa, has a mission history rich with examples of conflicting efforts and intentions in spreading the gospel message.

In 1738, German missionary George Schmidt, from the Moravian Mission, demonstrated a sincere and truthful proclamation of the gospel, settling among the Khoi people of the Western Cape. After seven years of ministry, including teaching the Khoi to read and write, he was forced

According to Michael Goheen, missional describes the purpose and identity of the church as it takes its place in God's story and participates in God's mission.[85] Alan Hirsch elaborates that the missional church takes its identity from, and organizes itself as God's instrument for, his mission.[86]

Barrett states that when missional is applied to the church, it is an ecclesiology with several essentials:

- The *missio Dei* 'creates the church and gives the church its reason for being' because God is missionary and sends his church out to the whole of creation.
- The missional church, because of its conformity to Jesus Christ, is above all an alternative or contrast community that is engaging with, while not conforming to, all that surrounds it.
- The missional church 'points to the reign of God' while at the same time depends on the constancy of God's actions, past, present and future.[87]

Tyra adds one more:

- The missional church is incarnational (versus 'attractional') because it is sent to deliberately engage with a 'postmodern, post-Christendom [and] globalized context'.[88]

## Missional leadership

In respect to this book, the term missional must also be applied to leadership in mission. To set the context, leaders of the church can be perceived as maintaining the church as an institution (that is, in the 'Christendom paradigm').[89] This is leadership by title and office, based on the Enlightenment concept of authority approved by the congregation.[90] This results in church leaders, especially ordained clergy, set apart to represent Christ to the people of God. Modern urban society has placed diverse managerial requirements upon church leaders, often expecting their churches to function as corporations. Leaders focus on managing the church as an institution and, in doing so, may uncritically borrow leadership models from spheres beyond the church. For example, church leadership models have arisen 'from psychology (counsellor, therapist), medicine (health and healer), the business world (strategist, coach,

to leave the Colony when he began baptizing converts. One of only five people baptized was a woman named Vehettge Tikkuie. Tikkuie persevered studying her New Testament, even after Schmidt was banished. Rooted in faith in Christ, Tikkuie kept the message of the Bible alive among the Khoi. Almost 50 years later, when Moravian missionaries returned to the area, they witnessed a thriving congregation of over 200 members, attributed to Tikkuie's continued ministry. She can truly be regarded as the first indigenous female evangelist in Southern Africa. Mission work among the Khoi succeeded, not merely because of human vessels such as Schmidt and Tikkuie, but because God fulfills his mission.

Another such example is found in Andrew Murray, born to 19th century Scottish missionaries to South Africa. Murray based and focused his life and ministry on our triune God. His legacy is a driving force that still today encourages South African mission involvement across the globe. According to Murray, 'The triune God is the Thrice-Holy One: Holiness is the deepest mystery of His being, the wondrousness of His righteousness and His love.'*

However, these types of success in mission were not always perceptible. Members of the London Mission Society (LMS) were often torn between the tension of serving and identifying with the oppressed indigenes, and upholding colonial order and civilization. By 1816, LMS missionaries were denied access to working with the local population, and some mission stations were closed down, all because of multiple charges of immoral and other inappropriate behaviors among the missionaries and those they came to serve. Despite the flaws in the messengers, the gospel continued to take root among indigenous communities.

Today, participants in Christian service face a world that is exponentially more complex than in Schmidt's or Murray's day. No more can one escape from or ignore global trends and realities that profoundly affect the local context.

One person who managed to navigate the complexities of both the Apartheid system in South Africa as well as prevailing global events is South African missiologist and theologian David Bosch. From his early ministry in 1957 forward, Bosch radically impacted global mission. His humility and integrity attracted even his adversaries, and his ability to clearly understand and articulate situations sets him apart as one of the most prominent missiologists of our time. Bosch helps us to recognize that

> we regard our involvement in dialogue and mission as an adventure, are prepared to take risks, and are anticipating surprises as the Spirit guides us into fuller understanding. This is not opting for agnosticism, but for humility. It is, however, a bold humility—or a humble boldness. We know only in part, but we do know. And we believe that the faith we profess is both true and just, and should be proclaimed. We do this, however, not as judges or lawyers, but as witnesses; not as soldiers, but as envoys of peace; not as high-pressure salespersons, but as ambassadors of the Servant Lord.[†]

Considering all this, what might the expression of mission look like if we return to the authority of the triune God in mission and remove the focus from the messenger?

[*] Andrew Murray, The Holiest of All: An Exposition of the Epistle to the Hebrews, 2004, Whitaker House
[†] David Bosch, *Transforming Mission: Paradigm Shifts in Theology of Mission*, 20th anniversary ed. (Maryknoll: Orbis Books, 2011), 500-501

manager), and the educational world (teacher)' and this is called the 'professional paradigm'.[91] When this happens, the role of church leaders may simply evolve to focus on satisfying the desires of 'spiritual consumers' in ways that do not represent missional leadership.[92]

As Christendom declines, the deliberate empowering of the people of God for mission is giving birth to a new paradigm of 'participatory leader'.[93] This model understands how the church's identity is found in participating in the triune God's mission. Missional leaders do not necessarily rely on a title for their authority and often operate through leadership teams where spiritual gifts are emphasized.[94]

Missional leadership understands how to nurture and release an innovative spiritual gift of leadership that has 'missional imagination' amongst the people of God.[95] The Holy Spirit uses his relational influence within the Trinity, and with the people of God, to oversee and cultivate the involvement of the whole community of God's people in God's mission. Therefore, missional leaders learn to understand the freedom of the Holy Spirit.

Additionally, missional leaders equip the people of God in interpreting the Bible for their contexts, developing an imagination for what God is doing, and making sense of their daily lives. In doing so, missional leadership must be courageous, equipped with biblical and theological minds and coupled with the ability to understand the changing cultural context.[96]

But why is it important to have common understanding around these terms of mission, *missio Dei* and missional?

Before we review insights gained from our survey of some theological developments around these terms, allow me this observation regarding our question: since the triune God is the perfect embodiment of hope, and the originator and source of mission, he calls and enables his people to be a community of the witness of his hope. Leadership-in-community then becomes a natural outworking of the ongoing expression of participating in God's mission.

## *Missio Dei*, Mission and Missional—a Review

- As its foundation and source, the *missio Dei* is the salvation activity of the triune missionary God. Jesus Christ is proclaimed, through the blood of his cross, as universal saviour for all. By this means God invites all people into the presence of his kingdom through new life in Christ. They become part of his community. God's will for his community, following the Holy Spirit wherever and whenever he leads, gives a preview of God's kingdom.

- While mission does not originate with or belong to the church, the triune God dispatches the church from where it is located, as his primary instrument—a sent community to carry out his mission to be his witness across the world in a broad spectrum of ministry. Consequently, mission is not restricted to the activity of missionaries sent by the church or other agencies who go overseas, crossing various barriers, to bring the message of salvation (with the caveat that 'missions' still means this in some circles).

- The church is a sign and symbol of the reign of God as it witnesses to the power of Christ through the transforming work of the Holy Spirit. Consequently, mission is holistic because it focuses on all of life and all of creation, calling people to abundant life. Through God's reign and its dynamic activity, a broken world spoilt by human sin and the powers of evil, is transformed into the new heaven and new earth of God's redeemed creation.

- Missional is an adjective describing something related to mission or something characterized by the mission of God. It demands one to be fully aligned to the mission of the triune God.

- Missional leadership is a paradigm shift from the Christendom concept of leadership through title and position, to the equipping of all God's people to live and serve in his mission. Missional leadership is transformational because it 'ignites and drives change' that is dependent upon the Holy Spirit. The focus starts with the 'inner transformation of the leader'.[97] This leads to the release of an innovative spiritual gift of leadership to lead and equip the transformation of God's people so they may effectively participate in God's mission in their particular contexts.

As we embark on a journey in the subsequent chapters examining complex global issues in this early part of the 21st century, we are reminded that our 'bold humility'[98] is anchored in the realization that 'we have this treasure in clay jars, so that the extraordinary power belongs to God and does not come from us' (2 Corinthians 4:7).

## Questions for Consideration and Discussion

1. Within the context of your small group, discuss what insights you have gained from the theological survey of the *missio Dei* presented in this chapter that are most relevant to your own ministry focus—or that of the team you're a part of.

2. In considering the scenario of the 'collapse of Christendom' in your context—and/or that of the church or agency you belong to—discuss in your small group how you would characterize your church or agency's leadership response or adaption to that.

3. Can you think of situations where you observe leadership-in-community in practice (even if not formally identified as such)? Is it a conscious response to the model we have in the Holy Trinity? Discuss within your group how your church or agency leadership might best bring awareness of the concepts presented in this chapter to a broader base of staff, members and partners.

## Questions for Consideration and Discussion

**CHAPTER 2**

# Globalization and Glocalization
# in the *Missio Dei*

I regularly read examples of individuals who hold power and authority, provided they have access to technology. It is commonplace, with a broadband connection, to run a global business from one's home, research any topic without ever visiting a library, arrange an overseas trip without seeing a travel agent, get a Bible college education without ever sitting in a classroom, or have an online conversation with a Hindu cleric without ever visiting a temple. I too work and live this way, and have done so since 2007 when I left my office at a mission headquarters. I conduct my global responsibilities from an office converted from part of my garage. My tools are a reasonably fast broadband connection, laptop and mobile phone. A lot of my research is done using Google Scholar and other online resources.

Globalization is uneven and can create barriers in language and communication. It is easy to assume that English is the official language of globalization. For example, in 2015 I was visiting the Wycliffe Japan team in Tokyo. Their Director met me at the Haneda airport and took me by three trains to where the office was, informing me that on the way back, I would be making the journey by myself. I decided that I should take photos of some of the key things I needed to do in order to purchase the right kind of ticket, get onto the correct train and get off at the right station, especially since all the signage was in Japanese. Three days later when I was ready to make my way back to the airport, I went to the first ticket machine and looked up the photo on my phone so I knew which buttons to press. But as I looked at the screen I noticed in the top right corner a blue button labelled 'English', so I pressed it. And of course, immediately all of the instructions, names of stations and so forth were in English. I didn't need my photo anymore.

Since I claim to be a Christian, I do have the Holy Spirit who is quite willing and able to point me in the right direction through God's word, his quiet whisper and godly input from other believers. But I'm not always listening or paying attention, and sometimes I stumble along wondering which 'button' to push, like at the ticket machine in Tokyo. Just like always wanting to get instructions in English, I can miss out on the language and message of the Holy Spirit—or worse—mindlessly 'convert' it to something that is easy for me. My challenge is how to integrate my dependence upon technology with a daily willingness to submit to the Holy Spirit's direction and leading.

An unhealthy dependence on the technological benefits of global-ization can mean that I rely less on others. The simple act of buying a train ticket meant I was more focused on the technology of my iPhone's camera rather than looking for some kind person to help me. This can be a 'dark' consequence of globalization when I stop appreciating other people. Yes, globalization at one level opens new vistas of opportunity. But those opportunities should not be a substitute for personal intercon-nection, first with God, and then with other people.

## Glocal is not Global Misspelled

Globalization and glocalization are relatively modern words, with the Herculean task of describing numerous interconnected concepts, actions, phenomena and real world consequences that nobody could have predicted even 40 years ago—at least not very well or holistically. And while historians can describe periods in time dating back centuries when global trade expanded via oceanic travel, for our purposes here, I am considering global shifts that have largely occurred within my lifetime.

Church and mission leadership needs to be acutely attuned to chang-ing global contexts. Church and mission movements are challenged to respond to effects of globalization and other factors, as these issues can-not be ignored.

Globalization has created unpredictable contexts, and leadership's swift adaptation is key to an organization's survival. This rapid and global state of change is due to the spread of technology, affordable air travel, global banking, virtual reality, rapid urbanization, and so on. Widespread availability and use of information technology continually disrupts the status quo of church and mission agency thinking. This may result in a fear of the future, which can paralyze leadership. Consequently, if leaders acting in God's mission aim to survive and thrive, openness to change is critical.

Consider these examples of issues—both global and regional—needing missiological examination here in the early part of the 21st century:

- The use of emotive slogans to drive the marketing of mission in a consumer oriented society;
- The trend toward reduction of world mission to a manageable enterprise, with an over-emphasis on research, statistics, quantifiable objectives and desired outcomes;
- The severe decay of a call to radical commitment and discipleship to Christ by large components of the church;
- An inadequate theology of suffering and martyrdom in terms of the mission mandate in the Western church (in contrast to the church across the globe);
- An emerging global culture that is focused on consumerism and materialism as a primary purpose of life;
- The significant erosion of a sense of urgency in mission—or the over-emphasis of urgency in mission to the exclusion of almost all else;
- Mega churches, with their size, influence and wealth, acting upon their own mandates, having the means to carry out mission virtually exclusively;
- Christians and churches being overwhelmed with information (about anything, including mission), and becoming disinterested about mission and what is happening in the world; and
- The general lack of understanding the missionary intentions of God and his church in the crossing of cultures in the local and global expressions of the *missio Dei*.

While some of the issues just noted are perhaps not immediately associated with globalization, I believe they all play out on a global stage. A careful look at key aspects of globalization—and later in the chapter, glocalization—can serve to better equip us in engaging with God in his mission.

## Globalization

A well-known description of globalization states that it is 'the intensification of worldwide social relations that link distant communities in such a way that local happenings are shaped by events occurring many miles away and vice versa'.[1]

At its heart, globalization has a number of core dimensions:

- It is powered by the interconnectedness of technological and economic factors where seemingly random developments in one part of the globe are affected by events in some other part of the world ;[2]
- It is enabled by broad economic advancement that embeds itself within the global context, allowing it to rely upon the free flow of trade, capital, information and labour across borders;[3]
- It pushes to extremes the progress of information technology which enables all manner of activity, such as the global transfer of financial investments;[4]
- It is a multidimensional process and interconnection that multiplies and intensifies social interactions,[5] and that creates 'shared social space';[6]
- It enables the exchange, integration and resulting consequences of human and non-human causes and activities across the globe;[7] and
- It is a political response to the rapid growth and expansion of the influence of the marketplace, both in the forms of dominance and marginalization.[8]

Globalization is not a recent construct; it has occurred, at least in the form of Western capitalism, since the late 19th century.[9] What was missing in that era is the rapid and inexpensive access to new infrastructures created by accelerating information technology and international travel. Thomas Friedman identifies three eras of globalization:

- From 1440-1800, Columbus's sea journey opened up trade routes and made the world seem a little smaller. The era was characterized by Western nations expanding their boundaries by claiming new territories far afield;
- From 1800-2000, the industrial revolution took place and multinational companies were able to develop global workforces and markets. The global economic engine opened up new trade relationships, fuelled by goods being moved cheaply and quickly across the world, by the growing presence of global banks, and by progressive governments removing financial barriers. The steam engine, railroad, telephone and airplane, followed later by the personal computer, satellite technology and the Internet, quickened the pace of development; and
- From 2000 onward, individuals or groups around the globe interacted with each other, without geographic location, language and culture as barriers. It is driven by widespread access to converging technologies, including the personal computer, smartphone, tablet, fiber-optic cable, faster mobile phone networks, widespread availability of Wi-Fi networks, improved software, diversity of apps, tools for social networking and powerful cloud computing. All of these innovations enable individuals to inexpensively access digital content from wherever they are located.[10]

Such a rapid development has led some to refer to the post-2000 world as being 'flat'.[11] Creators of this levelling state of affairs conceive of a world that follows a 'unified form of civilization' that was built upon Western Anglo Saxon cultural values.[12] However, globalization is not a 'one-directional... Western-managed process',[13] because Western societies have benefited as well from their interaction with nations of the global South and East, thus reflecting a global phenomenon. New players, not bound to one particular geographic or cultural context, continue to enter the global arena (e.g. China, India, Brazil, Indonesia, Mexico, Turkey, United Arab Emirates, and so forth), all made possible because of technological innovation and progress.

## Migration issues

Globalization has accelerated the migration of labour, as people move from one country to another in search of work and a better life.

The World Council of Churches (WCC) notes how the mobility of voluntary or involuntary migration has created a multitude of social and religious characteristics that affect the identity of individuals as they seek to settle within their new community.[14] Jehu Hanciles calls this 'deterritorialization (or delocalization)'. Its effects are dislocation from one's 'geographical space' and neighbourhood and all that is familiar (political allegiance, cultural identity, social relationships, and so forth) to what is totally unfamiliar.[15] This 'denationalization of social identity'[16] is one of the repercussions created indirectly by globalization and raises questions on the security of society because of this dislocation of people and their identity.[17]

This single issue of increasing global movements of people displays (sometimes in harrowing and heart-breaking ways) just how mindful leaders in global ministries need to be in terms of adjusting organizational strategies and responses.

## The English language

The English language plays an important role in globalization. It has standardized language in regions where a lack of a common language

1440–1800

**Friedman's Three Eras of Globalization**

impedes communication and trade.[18] While not the mother tongue of the majority of the world's inhabitants, English provides a unifying means for collaboration between nations in communications, information technology, trade, economics and so on. The widespread domination of English makes it the *de facto* language of globalization. Millions of people globally learn English, especially the American variety, so they can participate in a 'dynamic, pluralistic, and rationally innovative world'.[19]

## Technology

Advances in communications, transportation and technology demonstrate the startling speed of globalization. New technological advances quickly overtake current practices. Therefore, early adopters have a competitive advantage.[20]

The pace of early globalization quickened because tradable goods produced by blue-collar factory workers were delivered by 'hard infrastructure' (e.g. trains, ships, vehicles and airplanes).[21] Now, globalization is powered by 'soft infrastructure' (e.g. wireless technology and the Internet) that enables white-collar workers to be 'knowledge workers' who can operate from any time and any place.[22] This development, for example, has seen the company Apple become a powerful global brand with assets and reserves larger than many countries.

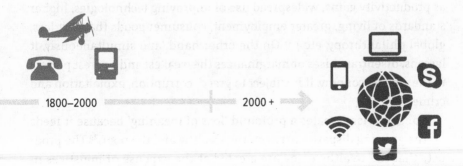

1800–2000          2000 +

## Urbanization

A result of globalization is the rapid pace of urbanization that benefits from technological and economic powers. Half the world's population lives in cities. By the year 2023, 750 million people will migrate to cities from rural areas.[23] By 2050, more than 70% of the global population will be urban.[24] The speed of urbanization is startling: globally, five million people a month are moving into sizable cities, and 16 million people a year are migrating from rural to urban China.

The great global cities of the world (e.g. London, Beijing, Tokyo, Hong Kong) have more influence over the global context than do many nation states. Not only is there huge population density, but there is also enormous financial, spiritual, and cultural influence. Because of their great diversity and financial, transportation and economic connections globally, cities like New York are 'a microcosm' of globalization.[25]

Globalization and urbanization make pluralism a characteristic of prominent cities of the world. Pluralism creates a situation devoid of a dominant culture. It occurs because global cities provide meeting grounds for people of all cultures, religions and worldviews.[26]

## Undesirable effects

The very nature of globalization is contradictory. On the one hand, it offers significant benefits and can be a powerful source for good (such as productivity gains, widespread use of improving technologies, higher standards of living, greater employment, consumer goods that cost less, global philanthropy, etc.).[27] On the other hand, and simultaneously, it lessens, disenfranchises or marginalizes the weakest and poorest players in the global economy. It is subject to greed, corruption, exploitation and crime.[28]

Consumerism creates a profound 'loss of meaning' because it feeds off the growing disparity between the wealthy and the poor.[29] The products that the wealthy enjoy are created at the expense of injustices in the labour pool of the developing nations, where worker conditions are often far from humane. The capitalist consumerism that globalization creates is imbedded with injustice and inequality. Consumerism is the Western world's 'most powerful *religious* movement'.[30]

The effects of globalization can take power away from local communities, or even nations, and place them into the global context. Most often, the effect is widespread resentment over the loss of control of one's life, the environment, jobs, the economy, the political system, and so forth.[31] Left unchecked, this leads to disorder and rebellion because people oppose what dominates them and they seek empowerment over their helpless situations.[32]

A mixed response to globalization is when for some, it is a new opportunity for prosperity; for others it only leads to conflict, out of control greed and ultimately can result in an indifference to the value of humanity.[33] The church, especially in the globalized consumer society, can become 'merely a vendor of religious goods and services', rather than an agent of holistic transformation.[34]

Globalization is not necessarily solving long held economic inequalities and political and religious differences. Instead, it brings social upheaval because of cultural and religious differences that defy integration or conformity.[35] This in turn develops into pluralism on the one hand, or tribalism on the other. It also fuels religious fundamentalism.[36] As a result, 'local nationalisms' arise in response to globalizing influences and tendencies, especially when the power of older nation-states fades.[37]

## Globalization and Christianity

Globalization is multidimensional. Not only does it affect politics and economics, it also influences culture and religion.[38] An effect of globalization on Christianity has seen it progress from being solely a 'Euro-American religion' to a global one.[39] The fact that the number of Christians in the global South and East now exceeds those in the West illustrates its global impact.

Religious groups, whether Wahabi Muslim, Pentecostal or fundamentalist Christians, have responded against globalization. This is particularly the case when the effects of globalization marginalize people, or if it encroaches on the influence of traditional religion and people's values.[40]

The US still plays a critical role in global mission even with the spread of the church into new territories, which is enabled by globalization. Robert Wuthnow thinks that statistical evidence of the growth of the church of the South and East is not the whole picture, because it does not indicate the obvious financial and people resources and global influence of the US church.[41] He is critical of Philip Jenkins' *The Next Christendom* for disregarding the on-going influence of citizens of the US as they lead missions, TV ministries, training institutions, not-for-profit humanitarian aid organizations, and so on.

## Pentecostalism and evangelicalism

Pentecostalism, due to its widespread acceptance, has become a significant medium for cultural globalization. This is based on observing the rapid growth of Protestant evangelicalism in places where, until recently, it has been unknown (e.g. Latin America, sub-Saharan Africa, and China).[42] The movement has developed local leadership and structures wherever it has gone; nonetheless, its leaders maintain close connections with evangelical centres in the US.[43] Even the use of American English within evangelicalism is significant. While at a local level, indigenous languages are embraced; at a national level, the assumption is that leadership will learn and use English to maintain contact with evangelical centres in the US.[44]

## Global South and East Christianity

Christianity has been 'an agent and a product' of globalization through the modern missionary movement of the 19th century onwards.[45] This spread of Christian beliefs from the Western world to the rest of the world established churches in new religious, linguistic and cultural contexts. This gave Christians, no matter where they were located, a new sense of identity, connection and belonging to a global body of believers.

By the year 2000, Western nations had large immigrant populations as total percentages. For example: France had 11%, the United States 12%, Canada 19% and Australia 25%.[46] This mass movement of people, most who come from the global South and East and move to the West, creates a growth of immigrant churches. Hanciles calls this the 'new frontier' of global Christianity.[47] Diaspora networks of missionaries, ministers or lay people from the global South and East who move and migrate around the globe create 'reverse mission'—mission from the diaspora into the new places they call home.[48]

### Multi-directional partnership

A benefit of globalization to mission is the creation of 'cross-cultural networking'.[49] As a result, any Christian can quite easily go overseas on a short-term mission trip. No longer is mission relegated to the professionals. Rather, globalization creates a vast and talented network of 'mission amateurs'.[50]

Globalization enables indirect and direct links between various churches and Christians in different countries.[51] This enables positive 'transnational and transcontinental partnership' in mission for the sending, training and deployment of missionaries.[52] On the other hand and as already noted, globalization creates economic and social inequalities that make such partnerships seem one-directional—from the wealthy West to the poorer rest.

## Glocalization

Globalization is 'unfeasible without localization' because of the juxtaposed relationship between global/globalization and local/localization.[53] The term 'glocal', derived from 'global localization', highlights this relationship.[54] While noting the causes and effects of our understanding that we are now citizens of the global world, simultaneously the processes of globalization provide means for developing the glocal cultural values that may facilitate harmony and overcome conflict.[55]

Glocalization can be traced to the Japanese business acumen of making products for a global market, but customizing them for local contexts.[56] This openness of a local context to foreign concepts is an indicator of its ability to glocalize. It is a dynamic, multifaceted and multidirectional relationship between the two.[57] In other words, it is how the 'local and modern' occurs alongside the 'global and Western'.[58] In addition, web based research into personal information allows merchants to direct their sales pitch locally to individuals.

## Examples

A global movement may have its broad appeal because it is able to readily adapt to a variety of local contexts. However, glocalization is evident when a local culture faces other stronger cultures and absorbs influences that are compatible to improve it, while repelling things that are truly foreign to it. For example, while English is the *de facto* language of globalization, the use of local languages on the Internet, radio and blogs is widespread because of the low cost of technology. All of this illustrates glocalization.[59]

An outcome of glocalization is how it safeguards cultural practices from being exported in their entirety to some innocent foreign context. Instead, glocalization creates the environment that promotes the imagination and strength of local communities to adapt and learn through the integration of the new ideas from 'transcultural relationships'.[60]

Lamin Sanneh states that the Bible's 'translatability' has a global-local dimension.[61] Bible translations are adapted to local contexts of any language and culture, demonstrating that God speaks in any vernacular. The Christian faith, according to Kwame Bediako, is 'the most culturally translatable' of all religions and faiths.[62] Bible translation is a primary contributor to Christianity's spread across the globe. Without Bible translation, 'the church would be unrecognizable or unsustainable'.[63]

Jenkins believes that Islam's desire to impose *Shari'a* law in places like Nigeria is a reaction to the perception of Christianity as a symbol of globalization and Westernization, as well as problems over liberal sexual issues.[64] However, Jenkins also notes that Christianity has always had a close relationship with poverty and that the typical Christian is 'unimaginably poor' by Western norms.[65]

Another example of glocalization is mobile (cell) phone technology. The mobile phone is increasingly considered to be a global communication tool. Although the majority of uses of the mobile phone are local, people can now talk to each other regardless of their location. Therefore, there is the 'nearness of use' (local), and yet at the same time, at least the perception of 'global reach'. Mobile communication does not eliminate the local, but simultaneously creates a 'new space' that is glocal.[66]

Perhaps an offshoot of glocalization is tribalism. As the world becomes more globalized, people will cluster in their families and communities—their tribes. Unchecked, tribalism can feed greater intolerance, sectarianism and militant nationalism.

| Some effects of **Globalization** | Some effects of **Glocalization** |
| --- | --- |
| Brings together information and knowledge from across the world | Safeguards cultural practices from exploitation |
| Gives widespread access to innovating and converging technologies | Enables local situations to adapt, learn and integrate new ideas |
| Enables problem solving through relational teams and their distributed intelligence | Assists in inherent tensions between global theologies and local contexts |

Some undesirable effects

| | |
| --- | --- |
| Subject to greed, corruption, exploitation and crime | Tribalism as a response to globalizing influences, which feeds intolerance, sectarianism and militant nationalism |
| Disenfranchises or marginalizes the weakest and poorest players in the global economy | Brings social upheaval because of cultural and religious differences that defy integration or conformity |

# Human Migrations in a Globalized World—an African Missiological Perspective

*by Mŭndara Mŭturi and Rahab Mŭndara*

One of the outcomes of globalization is the unprecedented movement of humans across cultural and political boundaries. News outlets show throngs of people seeking to cross borders and oceans as political and economic refugees, often exposing themselves to grave dangers and untold suffering. Immigration has become a divisive issue. Seeking an opportunity to survive or better their situation, desperate people are increasingly being met with hostility and rejection.

While the church adopts varying positions on immigration, scarcely have we as Christians looked at this issue from a missiological perspective, seeking to understand God's overall intentions on such population movements.

History is replete with incidents of human migrations. Throughout biblical times, from Abraham to Paul, God used migrations across cultures

## Theological influences have glocal impact

The general nature of globalization may affect the church in one part of the world, which in turn may unduly influence or override the church in another region. This intersection between global and local gives rise to the notion of 'glocalization'.[67] This term describes the mixture of the global with local manifestations, regardless of culture, practices, ideologies, and so forth. In other words, there is a 'blending' of the global and the local.[68] Therefore, glocal refers to how global and local interconnect. Glocalization is how people in one area navigate their relationship within globalization,[69] and it may provide a means for navigating the complexities of local contexts and reducing potential conflict between local and global.[70] In regard to complex issues of contextualization in the local church, the concept of glocalization may assist in the inherent tensions between global theologies and local contexts.

In my role as Executive Director of WGA, understanding the concept of glocal may also assist in interpreting how the church of the global South and East has different priorities and expectations concerning Bible translation than its Western counterparts. For example, Bible translation may be viewed as an integral part of the transformation of communities and not simply a stand-alone product for the church to use at its convenience. How do Western partners accept this? This requires thoughtful discussions to develop recommendations for the global church and mission agencies like WGA who are involved in the Bible translation movement.

## Leadership Response

Although it is apparent that church and mission agency leadership must respond to the unprecedented effects of globalization upon God's mission, should they act similarly to a CEO of a global company? It seems obvious that church and agency leadership must follow different criteria in adapting to and thriving in the necessary paradigm shift for missional structures.

Leadership in organizations with global outreach must to send out his people and establish his Kingdom on earth. At the height of European expansion between the 16th and 19th centuries, an estimated 60 million Europeans migrated to the New World of the Americas, Australia and New Zealand, and to newly created colonies in Africa and Asia. This period was also the peak of missionary enterprise.

Today, five of the top ten refugee-hosting countries of the world are in Africa: Ethiopia, Kenya, Uganda, Chad and the Democratic Republic of Congo. The church in these countries has not typically viewed refugees in missiological terms.

Traditional African communities are either settled or nomadic. Settled communities tend to be farmers, who value ownership of land, think in local terms, and are understandably concerned with seeking comfort and security. This can lead to a more isolated, inward-looking worldview, and can inhibit a global perspective.

Nomadic communities care little about ownership. They are concerned about survival, and view life from a broad perspective. Because of their migratory tendencies, they hold possessions lightly. They are often exposed to predatory circumstances, are acutely aware of the transience of life, and they behave accordingly.

Much like the settled African community, today's church across Africa is mainly local-minded, focused on ownership, comfort and security. The potential of travel abroad or emigration of its members is seen as an economic opportunity that could benefit the church with new wealth. Indeed, the church in the majority world of Latin America, Asia and Africa is producing Christian professionals and academicians that are as qualified as those from any other country. However, these gifted Christians are rarely taught in their home churches how to disciple others among their professional peers, and establish Kingdom values in the cultures in which they work. Instead, they tend to adopt values of their host cultures.

A more constructive way to prepare Christians who are departing Africa—whether sent out as traditional missionaries, leaving by choice, or relocating as economic or political refugees—is by modelling to them the example of the early church in Jerusalem. By training and discipling its members, the African church would likely see a missionary force arise, impacting and influencing cultures of the world with the gospel.

For many years, the African church has been a recipient of mission resources, both in people and finances. Through consequences stemming from globalization these resources have diminished, but preoccupation with local matters prevents the settled African church from fully recognizing the seismic changes taking place in global resourcing. A similar viewpoint from significant segments of the church in traditional funding countries has also changed, resulting in less resources coming to the local African context. This has led to some parallel patterns in churches in Africa—and all across the majority world—so that they too are restricting release of resources into missions work.

Fortunately, sections of the church in Ghana, Nigeria, Kenya and South Africa are responding to global church issues with local solutions and with much energy, which they are happy to share with the global church.

Churches in refugee-receiving countries do well to consider welcoming refugees as being faithful to God, by caring for them 'in a manner that pleases God' (3 John 1:5-6 NLT). Since God has brought these exiles to Africa, it's wise to ask how the African church can connect with them, conveying that which will last for eternity. Even further, we can understand our role as Daniel of the Bible did—to engage cultures and those who hold conflicting philosophies with Kingdom values.

continually cultivate respect for cultural diversity and manage change quickly, mainly due to technology and other globalization factors. Such leadership must manage complex information and situations in order to search for solutions. Leading in such a context requires building strong relationships across a multitude of boundaries, whether cultural, linguistic, geographic or organizational. Maintaining ethical and personal integrity is of paramount importance due to the diverse range of acceptable behaviours and practices in certain globalized contexts that may not be appropriate in one's own setting.

Readers may wonder (with good reason!) how on earth mission agencies and churches can appropriate and funnel energies toward a global mindset without degrading positive historical roots. In the next chapter, we'll explore the concept of polycentrism as applied to mission, and how acknowledging and allowing for multiple centres of influence across an organization can shine 'glocal lights' on global ministry.

## Questions for Consideration and Discussion

1. Early in this chapter there were nine issues listed that challenge churches and mission agencies, including: 'Christians and churches being overwhelmed with information (about anything, including mission), and becoming disinterested about mission and what is happening in the world'. Discuss in your small group or team how this may be happening in ministry situations you know of—and how leadership is addressing it.

2. As globalization continues to create both 'winners and losers' on the world stage, discuss in your small group or team how churches or organizations you know who are involved in overseas ministry foster/ develop a global mindset among their leadership. And if that is not the case, what factors do you think hinder such engagement?

# CHAPTER 3

# Paradigm Shifts and Polycentrism in the *Missio Dei*

In late 2007, when I began forming the leadership team of WGA, I deliberately sought out a cross-representation of experienced leaders from the global South and the West. I wanted women and men. I needed people who were global thinkers and knew how to act in complex situations. As the team was forming, we endeavoured to listen to the needs and opportunities of the organizations and people we serve from around the globe. We sought to become a catalyst for God's solutions into each of these complex situations.

Dr Ajith Fernando from Sri Lanka helped to further our process when he introduced the term 'inefficient lingering' in one of our leadership conferences in 2008. His concept is that more time should be spent in getting to know each other and listening to each other in an unhurried and relaxed setting. This can be a challenge if we're primarily focused on our own goals and strategies. At that conference, my wife Christine and I spent our meal and free times listening to stories from our friends and colleagues from around the world. For many it was the first time they had met Christine. They were glad to know that she really existed, since it was usually just me they had met in previous settings.

As I listened to the stories of our colleagues, what came to mind was the wisdom expressed by King Lemuel in Proverbs 31:8-9: 'Speak up for those who cannot speak for themselves, for the rights of all who are destitute. Speak up and judge fairly; defend the rights of the poor and needy.' Over the years that I have been in global mission leadership, I have often felt a responsibility to speak up for those from across the world because they were not being respected or welcomed to the 'table'. But I struggled with how to do that without becoming part of the problem.

Albert Einstein is attributed as saying that major problems or challenges we have do not get solved with the same level of thinking that created them. If Einstein is right, how do we look beyond our own strategies and structures to find solutions for the complexities of global mission? One way is to consider that the world has many centres of missional influence. This is our reality, and I thank the Lord for it.

One such centre of influence is Nairobi, Kenya. A few years ago I was invited to speak in a church of over 6,000 people in that great city. In my message, I challenged the leaders and congregation to take very seriously God's invitation to participate in his mission. I pointed out that they have received foreign missionaries for over 200 years. Now it is their turn to lead mission endeavours to nearby countries and beyond. This church had the resources to be a significant missional church to the nations.

There are similar churches across the global South and East. There also continues to be significant involvement of churches in the West in God's mission, and rightly so. All are needed in this intricately structured world. God blesses those who remind the church of the world's forgotten people. May our message continue to echo the words of the Apostle Paul: 'God chose things despised by the world, things counted as nothing at all, and used them to bring to nothing what the world considers important' (1 Corinthians 1:28 NLT). Thus, in the complex world we live in, the church is to be a humble instrument in God's mission.

## Paradigm/Shifts

Sometimes you don't fully grasp a concept until language evolves to give it context and a name. I doubt the Apostle Paul would have described what he wrote in 1 Corinthians as a world-altering paradigm shift, but there aren't many better examples than that. And, since it is God ordained, it lies outside the constraints of time and becomes applicable in any generation.

## Paradigm ...

Thomas Kuhn describes a paradigm as a set of assumptions, concepts, values, and practices that constitutes a way of viewing reality for the community.[1] When developed, it provides a useful tool to understand human perspectives and to describe sets of experiences, beliefs and values that affect the way people perceive reality and respond to it. Because paradigm shift is a theory, it can be temporary, and limited in the solutions it provides.[2] Nonetheless, it is a useful tool for exploring solutions to wide-ranging topics. This includes its usefulness to various missional practices.

## ... Shift

A paradigm shift takes place when a traditional or accepted perspective alters or converts to a new one. Kuhn describes the shift as a revolutionary change because of its radical characteristics as it responds to different realities.[3] No one creates the new paradigm single-handedly; instead the new one develops and matures over time. There are deep emotional reactions against the new paradigm until it is accepted.[4]

A crisis often triggers a paradigm shift. While the shift may require 'a radical conversion',[5] the crisis persists as long as it takes—years or even decades—before new achievements develop that lead towards the creation of a new paradigm.[6]

The resolution of the crisis is the emergence of the new paradigm. In this zone of transition the prevailing paradigm challenges the emerging one. The interim period is characterized by uncertainty and disorder.

Does this sound familiar? Maybe this 'zone of transition' describes a recent or ongoing scenario your church or agency is encountering. You would not be alone, and this phenomenon is worth looking at in some detail.

In the early stages of a paradigm shift, a lone individual with faith and courage must often take the lead in accepting it, because it is still unproven to the majority of the community.[7] Only after the new paradigm has been accepted and used does it prove trustworthy, because of its problem solving ability.[8] In order for this to happen, two conditions have to be met: (1) the new paradigm has to answer unresolved problems of the old paradigm; and (2) the new paradigm has to add to the 'concrete problem-solving ability' that existed in the old paradigm.[9] The shift is a complete change of direction, not an adjustment of the current path.[10]

Anne Schaef and Diane Fassel note the stages an organization goes through in a paradigm shift process: (1) letting go of the 'old situation and... identity'; (2) transitioning from the old through a 'neutral zone' to what is new; and (3) creating a 'new beginning'.[11] Others view this process as too mechanical and instead see the seed of the new thing planted very early on, usually when the current situation or relationship seems quite full. As a new idea grows, it develops within the existing situation, and often the two things are going on together with each demanding the same attention.

The history of science is a movement from one paradigm to another, each one simultaneously resisting and welcoming clusters of new information. Examples of such shifts in science include: the move from Ptolemaic astronomy (the Earth as the centre of the universe) to Copernican astronomy (the Sun as the centre of the universe with the Earth and

**Paradigm Shifts**

Often precipitated by a crisis

Interim/transition time is uncertain

Takes time before the new paradigm is accepted

Credible new paradigm is needed before the old is disused

Leadership encounters emotional reactions until the new paradigm is accepted

New may not completely replace the old

planets revolving around it); or the transition from Aristotelian dynamics (theoretical principles about the nature of reality and the primacy of the individual) to Newtonian physics (scientific and mathematical formulation of the laws of gravity). Each shift gave scientists tools for extensive debate before new concepts were deemed normative.[12]

## Paradigm shifts in theology and missiology

Although Kuhn's theory of paradigm shifts originated within science, Hans Küng applies the theory to theology, believing that the theory has similar applications from its use in science. For example, Küng notes: (1) as in science, theology also has authors, texts and proponents who demonstrate the ability to solve problems through the application of a growth of knowledge, and in doing so, observe a new paradigm taking place; (2) an historical observation of theology also points to places of crisis as a departure from the status quo resulting in new breakthroughs; (3) theology also experiences the old model being replaced by a new one; (4) theology also encounters a conversion to the new paradigm; (5) theology is also unsure whether new debates will result in new paradigms; (6) theologians also have crises of faith when they think they have been abandoned by all that they believed in; (7) a mixture of subjective and objective factors also plays havoc for theologians; (8) the early stages of a new paradigm in theology are accepted by only a few promoters; and (9) a new theological understanding may or may not be absorbed, replaced or set aside by the old one.[13]

These similarities give Küng confidence in identifying six models for interpreting the historical succession of Christianity, with a paradigm shift occurring between each one:

1. The apocalyptic paradigm of primitive Christianity;
2. The Hellenistic paradigm of the patristic period;
3. The medieval Roman Catholic paradigm;
4. The Protestant Reformation paradigm;
5. The modern Enlightenment paradigm; and
6. The emerging ecumenical paradigm.[14]

While these may be simplistic descriptions of tumultuous change within theological progression of Christianity, nonetheless, they provide a method for interpreting paradigm shifts in theology.

Fernando Canale observes that within each paradigm, Küng includes specific 'doctrinal, ecclesiological, sociological, political and cultural elements' that influenced how Christianity was understood in each epoch.[15] Bosch notes that Küng's divisions are very general, and because of the changing global context, the church must deal with various factors as it encounters a paradigm shift from Christendom to post-Christianity.[16] This is the crisis of mission that concerned Bosch:[17] after a thousand years of Christendom, the Western form of Christianity had lost its predominant place in global Christianity.[18]

In any season of paradigm shift in Christianity, Bosch observes the simultaneous effects of continuity and change.[19] This is marked by faithfulness to the constancy of past tradition and boldness to engage in future transformation.

What is the contribution and relevance of paradigm shift theory in relation to God's mission? The concepts of paradigm and paradigm shift, especially when applied to theology and missiology, provide a framework to interpret the changing context of the global church in the *missio Dei*, and how a new paradigm may already be under way.

Enough of theory. As noted at the end of Chapter 2, there is a significant working concept associated with globalization that can assist leadership navigating through—and beyond—organizational 'zones of transition'. That is polycentrism as viewed in the context of God's mission.

# Polycentrism

My chief means of experiencing this subject is through leadership within the WGA, among a diverse grouping of leaders from around the globe. Polycentric leadership was not a label we initially consciously proclaimed and sought to embrace—in fact the term can still strike me as a somewhat sterile descriptor for the living relationships that it references.

Instead, looking at polycentrism and over time juxtaposing it with issues stemming from paradigm shift, has been a much more organic process than what I could have imagined. Some reflection on this WGA process offers a peek inside a living laboratory.

## Polycentrism in WGA—some observations

By definition, the term polycentrism is the concept of allowing for self-regulating centres of influence within a singular structure. This occurs when there are many centres of power or importance within a political, cultural, or socio-economic system. The multiple centres may be of leadership, power, authority, ideology or importance within a larger 'political boundary'.[20]

Multiple centres of both growing and existing influences and places of spiritual vitality are impacting WGA—and many churches and global mission agencies—in positive and dynamic ways. Recall the story at the beginning of this chapter citing Nairobi as an example. These centres exist from Ethiopia to South Korea, from Papua New Guinea to Paraguay, from Singapore to South Africa—to name only a few. WGA welcomes and embraces such polycentrically informed and guided organizational leadership and direction setting.

An example of polycentrism at work is seen in WGA's evolution from having a centralized international institutional structure (beginning in the early 1990's), to becoming an alliance of 100 like-minded organizations with a decentralized hybrid structure. The benefit has been that the global church is more fully represented and engaged in what had previously been a predominantly Western institutional structure and paradigm devoted to Bible translation.

This hybrid structure of WGA forms a polycentric construct of many interrelating centres of leadership, which identify the vision for the WGA community, and find opportunities for its many organizations to make decisions, collaborate and act together in suitable ways. But as I began forming the WGA leadership team, there was no flowchart naming or illustrating polycentric leadership as a key response to a looming

## Community Empowerment

*by Nydia García-Schmidt*

In my role with WGA, I have had the opportunity to observe and listen to leadership and staff in a cross-section of churches and other organizations. Stemming from that, my understanding of community has broadened to include groups of people that may or may not be geographically connected, but who share interests, concerns or identities. To paraphrase urban policy analyst Peter Dreier, community empowerment involves mobilizing people to confront common challenges, and to strengthen their voice in institutions and decisions that affect their lives and communities.*

In a 2016 trip to Peru, I witnessed an example of the intersection of community empowerment and polycentrism in mission. I went to meet and interact with the Inter-ethnic Evangelical Association of Peru (ACIEP, Asociación Cristiana Interetnica del Perú), a relatively new association of nine organizations, founded in 2013, involved in Bible paradigm shift in the worldwide Bible translation movement. It grew into that. And like other things in life, sometimes you simply must begin a journey—and trust in the learning that comes along the way. In the case of polycentrism, fortunately there is a growing body of work revealing confirming elements relevant to leadership and organizations engaged in global mission.

### Polycentrism in socio-cultural situations

Polycentrism offers alternative viewpoints to parochialism (the assumption that one's belief or way of operating is superior to others) and ethnocentrism (one's assumed ethnic or cultural superiority). David Ahstrom and Garry Bruton comment that polycentrism is the opposite of ethnocentrism in that people try to do things 'the way locals do' or 'when in Rome, do as the Romans do'.[21] The end result can be that the local culture has the last word on matters such as the status of women or the acceptability of bribery, even if these issues may be in direct conflict with 'the parent firm or even homeland laws'. Caution is required, because adopting polycentrism without reflection could lead to 'ethical lapses' for participants.[22]

Balia and Kim observe that 'cultural polycentrism is a fact of our time', since cultural diversity is increasingly a global reality.[23] Polycentrism in inter-cultural situations is an 'awareness of otherness', which is an attitude of openness and curiosity that is willing to put aside both doubt about other cultures, and acceptance of one's own.[24] This is the ability to 'decentre' oneself as one takes on the 'perspective of an outsider' with their different set of beliefs, values and behaviours.[25]

Gary Bowen et al. suggest that informal and formal networks within a context operate like 'turbines' that are not 'centralized or pyramidal' in how they are governed, but instead, are polycentric with many interconnected centres of leadership. This provides 'social energy' for building capacity in the community.[26] Ron Hustedde states that polycentric leadership works well when it moves beyond team building to 'team learning', where leaders think collectively and learn to work in a coordinated way.[27]

translation, Scripture use and related ministries. ACIEP's mission is to 'promote Bible Translation and Literacy within the ethnic languages of Peru'. ACIEP currently represents work and ministry in about 27 minority languages of Peru, mostly Quechua speakers, estimated to number four and a half million.

Participating in this meeting was like walking into new territory. I didn't know what to expect, except to be expectant, knowing that anything could happen. One participant said, 'I've never heard of Wycliffe Global Alliance. Who are you guys? Where are you coming from?' The concept of global mission and their connection to it wasn't yet there for them. As the meeting progressed, the ACIEP participants got a better understanding of other networks and groups not unlike themselves engaged in Bible translation around the world. Perhaps most importantly, they were grasping ACIEP's own involvement and significance in the bigger picture, and that without their input, a key voice would be missing from the global conversation.

As I listened to ACIEP's staff, it was clear that they had a strong ownership for the part they played in making God's Word accessible to their communities. They spoke in great detail about ensuring that their work was actually having the desired impact. I could identify among them both men and women who were problem solvers, visionaries, leaders, paradigm shifters, strategic thinkers and community builders. When presenting some WGA principles about community, and Biblical foundations for the work of Bible translation, I began to sense a revitalized outlook among them. All these signs demonstrate aspects of community empowerment.

The ACIEP team had questions about how to work more effectively as an association, and how to bring what they were learning to their own Peruvian community leaders. They talked about the importance of developing better representation with government officials, because Quechua-speaking communities may not understand or readily accept some government policies. ACIEP's leadership realized the need to become stronger and more effective in their context. The members of ACIEP were happy to know that they had a space and a voice, not just in their local situation, but also in the global scenario.

Near the end of our time together, I asked the ACIEP leadership and all who were participating in the meeting to consider what they could contribute to the larger Bible translation movement—a question they had not been asked before. Then they debated among themselves how to include more organizations and people in their association—mainly because they found value in creating capacity for others.

ACIEP is one of many emerging polycentric centres of influence realizing the important role they play in developing sustainable and contextualized approaches to taking God's word to their own indigenous communities. In addition, they increasingly understand how their voices and experiences are vital for the larger mission movement. By embracing the values of affirming and nurturing polycentric communities, a participatory approach is fostered between global and local, recognizing that community empowerment is acting upon this vital inter-linkage—regardless of the nature of the ministry focus.

* Peter Dreier, "Community Empowerment Strategies: The Limits and Potential of Community Organizing in Urban Neighborhoods." *Cityscape* (1996): 121-159.

## Polycentrism in organizational leadership contexts

Some theorists, such as Ori Brafman and Rod Beckstrom, provide analogies for centralized leadership structures (e.g., a spider) and decentralized leadership structures (e.g., a starfish).

In a centralized structure it is clear who is in charge, with a specific place where 'decisions are made' (i.e., the corporate headquarters or the board room). This leadership is 'coercive', because the leader holds ultimate power and authority and 'uses command-and-control to keep order'.[28] This coercive arrangement depends on hierarchy, like a pyramid in structure, where someone is always in charge.[29] The organization is divided into departments, which act as silos, separate from each other. These are the legs of a spider and when it is functioning well, each leg does its job and supports the organization. However, cut off the head of the spider and it dies. The analogy is the same with a hierarchical structure—without the CEO as the head, the organization will move into decline and eventual organizational death.

In contrast, an open or decentralized organization is 'amorphous and fluid'.[30] Knowledge and power are dispersed and this creates great flexibility as entities respond quickly to any type of situation by 'spreading, growing, shrinking, mutating, dying off, and reemerging'.[31] This structure operates like a starfish, because it does not have a head that gives central commands, and its main organs are duplicated throughout each of its arms, since it is actually 'a neural network' that functions as a decentralized system.[32] Just as with a starfish, a decentralized organization can lose a leg or two and still survive, but with all legs working well together, a decentralized organization can be highly effective.[33]

Informal organizational structures have been thought to have limitations. However, in the 'absence of structure [and] leadership', there is an advantage: It is ideology rather than structure that is the essential glue that holds the decentralized organization together—the 'fuel' that drives the decentralized organization.[34]

While a decentralized structure may tend to appear 'ambiguous and chaotic', it still may achieve measurable results.[35] The measuring criteria, however, are different: how active are the circles of networks, are they distributed, are they interdependent, and do they bring new kinds of connections between them?

Suzanne Morse claims that a structure that is neither centralized nor decentralized is therefore polycentric.[36] This is a hybrid model with a 'bottom-up approach of decentralization', but with at least some degree of control and structure of centralization.[37]

## Polycentrism in missional movements

JR Woodward believes that hierarchical forms of leadership create 'an individualistic approach to spiritual formation', whereas polycentric leadership provides 'a community of leaders within the community'.[38] This is especially relevant amongst the Millennial (born in the 1980s-1990s) and Digital generation (born after 2000) where 'cultural architects' equip others in the community.[39] The cultural architect creates a missional culture that enables 'the priesthood of all believers'.[40]

The polycentric model of missional leadership gives people 'equal authority and revolving leadership' as they pursue community and 'wholeness together'.[41] Spiritual maturity is modelled by an interdependent community of leaders with their various strengths and weaknesses, who are open and transparent to others in the community. This is in contrast to the pastor who is expected to function with the same level of authority as the North American business world CEO model where merits and performance are associated with the role.[42]

## Polycentrism and the global church

The past one hundred years of growth of the global church has birthed, according to Balia and Kim, 'a polycentric world church'.[43] Klaus Koschorke suggests that the various epochs in the history of World Christianity should also be viewed as polycentric movements. Throughout church history has been the plurality of centres of the church, cultural expressions of Christianity, confessional variations, and 'indigenous initiatives' of the emerging churches.[44]

Koschorke cites Ethiopia as an example of polycentrism in church history. The Ethiopian church claims its biblical origins dating back to King Solomon. Ethiopians have had their own biblical Canon, their own liturgical language called Ge'ez', differing church customs with their practice of the Sabbath and of circumcision, and unique structures of the church. The Ethiopian king resisted the onslaught of missionaries from Europe in 1881 'on the grounds the Ethiopians were already Christians'.[45] Ethiopia in colonial times was also the only African country to resist European colonialism when the Italian army attempted an invasion in 1896. Consequently, Ethiopian Christianity had a great impact upon the African elite of the 19th century because it inspired them to be 'religiously-modern' (meaning Christian), without desiring to become dependent on Western missionaries. It was as though the word 'Ethiopia' became 'a symbol of political and ecclesial independency' because it was 'black, it was free, and it was Christian'. These matters influenced the churches of African Americans, the Caribbean and parts of sub-Saharan Africa.[46]

Another example is with the development of diaspora churches in Western countries that originated from the global South and East. Through extensive migration, Christians from the global South and East bring new examples of theological education and formation to the West. The outcome is theology that is better suited for the challenge of mission in the West as the Western church learns from the churches from the global South and East. Thus, Christianity can be viewed as polycentric because it has many 'cultural homes' within a diversity of contexts and is not permanently attached to any particular one.[47]

Western influences of the church are transmitted globally because of a disparity of power such that the receiving context becomes dependent upon the Western church. The Ethiopian example is why leadership from the global South and East must be enabled to provide a balancing influence on Western mission strategy. This is possible through a polycentric missional leadership.

The polycentrism of cultures and languages provides a reason that the Bible's translatability has been a vehicle for the spread of Christianity across the globe, demonstrating that it is 'at home in all languages and cultures, and among all races and conditions of people'.[48] According to Sanneh, 'Christianity has developed as a "vernacular" faith' to the extent that each person with a Bible in their mother tongue 'can truly claim to hear God speaking to us in our own language'. Sanneh elaborates:

> Being the original Scripture of the Christian movement, the New Testament Gospels are a translated version of the message of Jesus.... The issue is not whether Christians translated their Scripture well or willingly, but that without translation there would be no Christianity or Christians.[49]

## Polycentrism and Leadership-in-Community

The point for delving into polycentrism, and for that matter, paradigm shift, at this juncture in the book, is partly to bridge into the next chapter's topics: friendship and community.

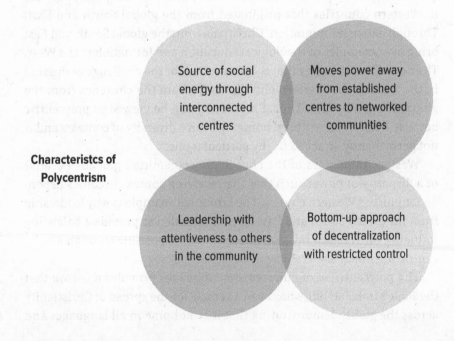

**Characteristcs of Polycentrism**

Source of social energy through interconnected centres

Moves power away from established centres to networked communities

Leadership with attentiveness to others in the community

Bottom-up approach of decentralization with restricted control

Polycentric leadership enables more of a communal approach where leaders operate within an array of interconnected communities. Through polycentrism, there is a deliberate attempt to move away from established centres of power, so that one leads from among others. In this way there is creative learning as leaders and friends in community, with attentiveness to others, and increased leadership and influence from the margins (real or perceived) of the global church.

Polycentrism applied to global missional leadership provides a purposeful shift from the Christendom concept of leadership through title and position, to the equipping of all God's people to live and serve in mission across various centres of power.

## Questions for Consideration and Discussion

1. Early in the chapter, the phrase 'zone of transition' was mentioned as possibly describing a recent or ongoing scenario your church or agency is encountering because of organizational paradigm shift. Using examples you're aware of, discuss among your small group what that transition looks like.

2. Discuss in your small group if you think polycentric leadership could be useful in your church or organization. If this dynamic is already evolving in your context, share what is helping or hindering the process.

# CHAPTER 4

# Friendship and Community
## in the *Missio Dei*

Within the Bible translation movement there's often an emphasis on statistics. Counting the progress of how many languages now have the Bible, or how many new Bible translation programs were started in a given year, is very important to our cause. Throughout the modern missionary movement we have used statistics as an indicator of whether or not progress is being made.

There is another aspect of mission that is much more difficult to measure: the state of friendship and collaboration amongst churches and mission agencies. This 'measurement' calls for an emphasis on building healthy relationships of trust and mutuality as friends in God's community.

The importance of friendship really took hold of me when I hosted a small consultation of Western mission leaders with church and mission leaders from Africa. We met in Addis Ababa, Ethiopia, in 2014. Over two days we shared with each other our personal stories as we took the time to get to know one another. We had no other agenda than to explore what friendship looks like from biblical, theological and missiological viewpoints. This was an enriching time for all of us. It especially impacted me because it reinforced a growing conviction that this was a missing yet important foundation for participating in God's mission.

During the consultation, we explored Bible texts such as Proverbs 18:24, 'there is a friend who sticks closer than a brother'; or how Abraham's faith in God meant that God called him his friend (James 2:23); or we are Christ's friends when we do what he commands us to do (John 15:14). Studying these and other related texts strengthened my conviction that we have to be committed to friendship, and this has missional impact because friendship between people of all socio-economic, religious and other class differentiations gives God glory and serves as a visible demonstration of God's kingdom.

C.S. Lewis stated that, 'Friendship is unnecessary, like philosophy, like art... It has no survival value; rather it is one of those things that give value to survival.' In many cultures the value of friendship is paramount. For example, in 2015, I facilitated a discussion at a retreat of the staff of the Papua New Guinea Bible Translation Association. One of the topics was 'Friendship in God's Mission'. I asked the question: 'What unique values of friendship do Melanesians bring to the regional and global Bible translation movements?' The participants gave dozens of ideas. I asked them to agree on just five 'gifts' that they would offer to the regional and global church and missional movements. They settled on these: (1) gift giving without an expectation of something in return, so that friendship is strengthened; (2) friendly greetings first before anything else; (3) developing relationships first before focusing on a task; (4) visiting friends so as to be available to listen and support; and (5) sending out trained Papua New Guineans to contribute to the Bible translation movement, within the region and beyond. Noticeable is their emphasis on relationship and friendship.

I am convinced that if we make friendship in community an emphasis, God's mission is better served. Statistics do matter, but healthy and thriving relationships amongst God's people are of the greatest consequence.

## Friendship in Mission

Friendship within the triune God sets the example of divine and human friendship. An intimate relationship with the triune God in community and friendship with others forms the most basic foundation for mission.

That sounds like the right thing to say in a book like this. And it is. But many of us, if we're honest with ourselves, examine our busy ministry schedules and sometimes feel remorse about not finding enough time for friends. Which is of course mildly ironic—as that sort of heartfelt emotion is exactly the type of thing to share with friends. But a blessing of friendship is that it's mutual. It is recognition at a deep level that we are not alone.

This review of friendship in God's mission aims to provide insights into why the topic is of relevance to the development of a global missional mindset.

## Theological basis

The Gospel of John is rich in 'the vocabulary of friendship'.[1] For example, John the Baptist is portrayed as the 'friend' of the bridegroom (John 3:29); and Martha, Lazarus and Mary as Jesus' friends (John 11). In John 15:13, Jesus states that when a person gives his/her life for a friend, this is the ultimate expression of love. He then says (15:14-15), 'You are my friends if you do what I command. I no longer call you servants.... Instead, I have called you friends...'. Jesus addresses a 'community of friends', who for the apostle John, are all who are in the 'community of faith'.[2]

The basis of Jesus as the ultimate friend can be understood as his commitment to his friends, in the same way that his friends are committed to him, and show this by their resolve to walk in his ways. Nancy Bedford points out that this is where Jesus' language is Trinitarian: 'I have called you friends, for everything that I learned from my Father I have made known to you' (John 15:15). Bedford suggests that friendship with the triune God is a relationship that transcends 'that of servant... and even... children of God'. The implication is 'gratitude for God's friendship' is lived through friendship with others.[3]

How Chuang Chua observes that the triune God sets the example of friendship through his invitation for his followers to participate with him in his 'relational life' by calling people to a friendship, first with him and then with others. This invitation to friendship, divine and human, forms what Chua claims is the most fundamental or 'primordial missiological principle'.[4] Further, it was the event of Christ coming and 'reconciling the world to himself' (2 Corinthians 5:19) that created the opportunity for a new and permanent relationship with the triune God and humanity since all are 'invited into God's presence and friendship'.[5]

# Being, Doing, Beautiful!

*by Susan Van Wynen*

N
o one was talking about John 17 back then. Well, at least no one I'd been listening to.

Fifteen years ago, while working on strategic planning, I happened to read John 17. It was a mental 'drop everything!' moment when I read

that all of them may be one, Father, just as you are in me and I am in you. May they also be in us so that the world may believe that you have sent me. I have given them the glory that you gave me, that they may be one as we are one—I in them and you in me—so that they may be brought to complete unity. Then the world will know that you sent me and have loved them even as you have loved me. (John 17:21-23)

'May they also be in us so that the world may believe...that they may be brought to complete unity. Then the world will know...' Wait a minute—*this* is The Strategy! When

## Missiological basis

Dana Robert maintains that the yearning for cross-cultural friendships provides a significant incentive for mission because practitioners see developing 'interracial and intercultural relationships as both a means of mission and an end in itself'.[6] In addition, Jooseop Keum notes that faithful mission takes place in the interchange of 'life and action' through an approach of 'respect and friendship' that involves a deeper 'listening to others'.[7]

Following on with this idea of dialogue, Balia and Kim contend that interaction with others from different backgrounds (such as religious, socio-economic, cultural, and so forth) is of foremost importance in developing relationships in mission.[8] It is the pathway to creating friendships across all types of barriers.

Looking back over 100 years ago to the 1910 World Missionary Conference in Edinburgh, one is reminded of the importance of friendship. Through the close friendship with Western leaders Sherwood Eddy and John Mott, a young Anglican minister from India named Samuel Azariah

(1874–1945) was invited to participate in the conference. He was one of only about 20 representatives from the global South and East.[9] Speaking to the conference, Azariah said:

> Missionaries, except for a few of the very best, seem… to fail very largely in getting rid of an air of patronage and condescension, and in establishing a genuinely brotherly and happy relation as between equals with their Indian flocks…. You have given your goods to feed the poor. You have given your bodies to be burned. We also ask for *love*. Give us FRIENDS![10]

The call for friendship in mission from Azariah is remembered as one of the most noteworthy statements from the Edinburgh 1910 World Missionary Conference. And yet, a century later, the church is still burdened with 'friendships strained by post colonialism, dependency, paternalism and poverty'.[11]

Azariah was committed to cross-cultural friendship because he personally observed its power. In his second address at the

we are in Him we can be in complete unity. Then the world will sit up and take notice that something's different here, and acknowledge Him.

But this isn't a strategy we can *do*. It's about *being*, and then the *doing* naturally flows from that *being*. That's where friendship and community enter in.

Friendship—that word can mean many things and take many forms. In some cultures friendship and business are kept separate. In others, you don't do business if you don't have the friendship. For some, friendship means loyalty, no questions asked. For others, there are strong ties to reciprocity. True community and unity only become possible when we start to reflect on and practice biblical expressions of friendship.

Community is not the same as collaboration, though we often mistake collaboration for community. Collaboration can be a good way to accomplish something together, but it's not a good start for a true relationship. When relationships are built around task, what happens when the task is over? Or, what happens when plans go awry? What happens when one partner in the collaboration gets the desired result, but another partner doesn't? It is only when collaboration and partnership are grounded in true community that we can see and experience what God intends.

In my early enthusiasm in leadership roles, I made some assumptions: I assumed the Christian colleagues I was serving with were already friends. I assumed these friendships would be a sufficient start for new ways of both being and doing. I assumed that with enough good will and collaboration we'd have that desired unity. And I assumed that somehow the world (or at least some portion of it) would notice. I could not have identified and articulated all these assumptions back then, but I've learned the hard way—and I'm still learning—the disadvantage of making such assumptions.

Many of my colleagues would have considered themselves to be great friends at a personal level, but in the work place, assumed expectations of stakeholders took precedence over assumed personal friendships. But what could have emerged if we'd all sat down and had an actual conversation together? When assumptions are set aside, there is ample space for true relationships to grow. And when relationships grow, boundaries dissolve.

However, even well intended personal (or transactional) friendships can't reach the depth and breadth God can reach through transformational friendship. I've often heard talk about being committed to the task or to partnership or collaboration, or even to mission. But it is not as common to hear talk about commitment to each other and to the Body of Christ. That's community, and it grows out of our relationship and friendship with God and with each other.

I've seen it in action, the being and the doing. Friends, serving Christ in true community. And it is beautiful. It's beautiful because it is not of our making. God created us for community. It's beautiful because we can participate in it with Him, in all our diversity, and with all our flaws. It's beautiful because it displays the unity to which He has called us. And it is beautiful because it draws the world, not to us, but to Him.

conference, Azariah pleaded his case for a visible demonstration of the Christian vision of God's kingdom to his fractured Indian society, divided by caste and structural injustice. His country needed to witness how the church was bound 'together across the dividing lines of caste, ethnicity, culture and empire' by a unique quality of friendship 'derived from the knowledge... of the exceeding riches of the glory of Christ'.[12]

Racism and missionary paternalism have been one of the chief barriers to the Christian life. To overcome this requires 'all races working together' so that the full glory of Christ is achieved, because 'only cross-racial friendships... reveal the image of the Lord'.[13] Since economic polarities and social inequalities still exist within the global church, Azariah's fervent plea is still relevant.[14] By identifying failures in human relationships as the most fundamental of all missionary failures, Azariah hit upon a 'raw nerve' in Western Christianity.[15]

Robert notes that 'world friendship' was a forceful philosophy that came out of the 1910 Conference.[16] Some Western missionaries have followed this pattern with those from the global South and East, who regard friendship as a core value. To some degree, after the 1910 Conference, friendship became a compelling principle in the spread of Christianity 'as a multicultural community', because friendship demonstrated Christ's love that helped overcome the inequalities and 'racism of the colonial era'.[17]

## Partnership supplanting friendship: the need for a third space

Towards the end of the 1950's and coinciding with the ending of European colonialism, a new vocabulary of 'partners, partnering and partnerships' superseded the theme of friendship in mission as the appropriate 'ethic for a postcolonial age'.[18] Into this milieu Janice Price calls for a 'third space', one that is between the West's new colonialism with its 'domination of resources [and its] cultural hegemony', and those in the global South and East who live without the power and influence of financial resources.[19] This third space is a renewed call for making friendship in mission an important commitment.

Price's observation can be illustrated in this way:

### The First, Second and Third Space

| First Space: | Third Space: | Second Space: |
|---|---|---|
| Western colonialism and domination of financial resources and cultural hegemony | Commitment to Friendship in Mission | Global South & East without power and influence of financial resources |

Robert observes that 'Azariah's cry' was both a protest and a 'prophecy'. Real friendship across 'widening economic divides' is difficult but possible. True cross-cultural friendship requires a long-term commitment between individuals and places and includes the need to understand, respect, learn from, and live amongst another culture or religion. Robert concludes, 'despite the dangers of unreflective paternalism, friendship remains the proof and the promise of Christianity as a multicultural, worldwide religion'.[20]

## Implications

A missiology of friendship creates a greater openness to others by walking and serving humbly as friends with Christ and each other. In my leadership role, I have considered some implications of this for WGA in the form of several questions. It may be of interest as you read these questions to substitute your own church or organizations' particulars in place of 'WGA' and 'Bible translation movements'.

1.  Changes continue to take place in Bible translation movements with new players who are seeking to listen to and discern the movement of the Spirit; do organizations in the WGA community believe that all participants in Bible translation movements are essential?

2.  It is possible that WGA's strategies and structure obstruct others who should be involved; are there ways in which WGA is leading that hamper the participation of others in Bible translation movements?

3. WGA must be cautious not to appear as an authority or expert to others in Bible translation movements; is WGA willing to take a humble attitude and seek to learn and change its perspectives when necessary?
4. Is WGA willing to let God redefine how he wants it to participate in his mission?

With those important questions serving as a backdrop, we now move into the area of community in mission. In a very real sense, the entire framework of this book can be traced to one aspect of community or another. Acknowledging the wealth of published material about Christian community, for purposes of this chapter, I will briefly relate some foundational understandings of community as it pertains to developing a global missional mindset.

## Community in Mission

Community is defined as 'a social, religious, occupational, or other group sharing common characteristics or interests and perceived or perceiving itself as distinct in some respect from the larger society within which it exists'.[21] Sharing common characteristics at a larger scale is what binds together all manner of communities. Frances Hesselbein et al. suggest that at the global level, community is actually 'a series of communities that are interdependent and diverse, embracing differences, releasing energy, and building cohesion'. The larger global community is 'enriched by the health of the many smaller communities' that comprise the whole.[22]

The concept of community in mission may be somewhat countercultural, going as it does against values of independence. Therefore, some considerations concerning its importance include the following:

- It starts with the desire for any mission movement or structure to become a community of trust, with friendship as an expression of the unity of believers;
- Community is essential in mission, and relies upon the spiritual transformation of leaders and the community they lead;
- Harmonious inter-cultural relationships are required, because

working in community is essential. God's desire is for resources to be willingly, readily and generously shared through the community of God's people, so that all may benefit; and

- Community is dependent upon God's grace, because the work of the cross is the ultimate equalizer among people.

### Characteristics of a Healthy Community

Values are deeply embedded in the community

Resources are willingly and readily shared through the community

Inter-cultural friendships are valued

An inter-generational and inter-cultural mix creates a nourishing community

A thriving community is transformational

Promotes harmonious inter-cultural relationships

## Community as an expression of *missio Dei*—a living example

From an organizational leadership viewpoint, it is not always easy to translate a preferred 'state of being' for a mission agency or church when it comes to a concept like community in mission. As ministry engagement expands—especially, but not exclusively, in multi-cultural scenarios—it is beneficial to bring awareness to what an increasing sense of community means for an organization. This is an ongoing process and reflects the value of life-long learning.

Drawing once more from my experience in WGA, in 2011 our leadership sensed the need for strengthening values of community within and between the organizations that formed WGA. It was determined to convene a small gathering of WGA leaders in Accra, Ghana, in 2012 to discuss the topic of 'Community within WGA as an Expression of *Missio Dei*'. One example of what eventually transpired was the formulation of the WGA *Principles of Community*.

The principles were developed through a missiological consultative process—a process discussed fully in chapter 5. They are based upon these four foundational statements:[23]

1. 'We are created for community and called to community': The triune God is a 'loving, honouring community'[24] because it is the 'relational family of three divine Persons in one eternal essence',[25] each in communion with the others. The eternal existence of God 'has been in community'.[26] This is the relational character of God as expressed in the Trinitarian nature of God himself. Therefore, just as there is relationship amongst the Father, Son and Holy Spirit, this becomes the model for relationship amongst God's people.

2. 'We are God's people, called to consistently and lovingly relate and behave according to the instruction of His Word and the example of Christ': As God's people relate to each other in community, their individual and mutual spirituality is strengthened. This has missional impact, because it fulfils Jesus' desire for the unity of community as a witness to the watching world (John 17:23).

3. 'Living and serving in community glorifies God and provides a tangible example of the Gospel in action. We reflect the image of God through intentionally modelling authentic community': The church is the community of Jesus' disciples, the community of servants, and the 'community of ministry'.[27] Christ therefore sends it out into the world. God's very nature is 'communitarian', and therefore his mission is 'a divine community effort'.[28] The church is God's community because 'it is a network of relationships' where each person has responsibilities for each other.[29]

4. 'A community that glorifies God attracts people to God and His mission': God who is self-giving created the human community in his image to also be 'self-giving' and to be part of a self-giving body, the church. Christians give of themselves to others in order to 'fulfil [their] God-given design'.[30]

It is important to point out that the WGA *Principles of Community* were not formulated at the Accra consultation. What took place in Accra was an initial exploration of biblical, theological and missiological factors relating to community. This then led to wider discussions across WGA in both formal and informal settings about the theme of community. It was from these wider discussions that the impetus to formulate some principles took hold in 2014—with the understanding that any resulting principles document would be considered a living document, allowing for continued input.

This period of three years from WGA leadership's recognition of addressing this issue (2011) to publishing a set of living principles (2014) is in itself a reflection of the value of community.

## Community as Congruence

Mūndara Mūturi, long time WGA leader from Kenya, expresses the significance of community this way: We become 'like a big river [with] individuals and organizations coming in convergence or confluence and pooling resources for Kingdom purposes. Individuals and autonomous organizations disappear in the congruence of community.'

I would add that it is from this posture that we learn to look beyond our own needs and self-interests to see others. We do not disappear into a nebulous mass that one then calls a community, and we don't lose self-awareness. What we gain is increased awareness of our friendship and fellowship with the triune God.

···  ···

# Questions for Consideration and Discussion

1. In the context of your small group or team, discuss how friendship and partnership are expressed at an organizational level in your agency or church. As individuals, provide any particular examples, and ensure that everyone in your group has opportunity to give feedback and/or provide their own examples.

2. Discuss with others in your small group or team any instances when you have felt the sensation of being an outsider while overseeing or directly engaging in core ministry activities in your church or mission agency. Let all who want to participate take a turn. Simply listen to each other's stories.

3. Consider any impending situations in your own organization, church or mission agency when there may be opportunity to bring increased awareness to the value of community and friendship-in-mission. Discuss any conditions that may help or hinder such opportunities.

## Questions for Consideration and Discussion

1. In the context of your small group or team, discuss how friendship and partnership are expressed at an organizational level in your agency or church. As individuals, provide any particular examples, and ensure that everyone in your group has opportunity to give feedback and/or provide their own examples.

3. Consider any impending conditions in your own organization—church or mission agency—that prevent the opportunity to bring increased awareness to the value... from your organization's on-mission. Discuss any conditions that may help or hinder... opportunity...

# CHAPTER 5

# Reflective Practitioners and the Consultative Process in the *Missio Dei*

In 1999, I was appointed as the Executive Director of Wycliffe Australia. It only took a few months before I started wondering if I needed a working understanding of how missiology could contribute to my leadership. I didn't have any ambition to become a missiologist, nor was I sure that a study of religious missions, their methods and purposes was relevant to modern mission leadership.

However, the more I met with church, mission and Bible college leaders in Australia, the more I realized something was missing on my side of the conversation. I was lacking confidence in some areas but I couldn't pinpoint what they were. What I did know is that I was more interested in the task, ministry goals and results than I was in having a working theology of mission and applying that to leading the ministry.

Then I met Les Henson, senior lecturer in mission studies at Tabor College in Melbourne. It didn't take long for Les to convince me that he could help me. So I enrolled in the Bachelor of Arts study program that he tailored for me. It was a risk, as I wasn't sure this field could be useful to a leader of a Wycliffe organization.

At the first class I discovered that most of my fellow students were little more than half my age, just preparing to be missionaries, and to do so had embraced the field of missiology. Together, we worked through subjects such as a theology of mission, mission history, contextualization, world religions, and so forth. As I began learning, while still working fulltime in leadership, I quickly saw the relevance of my studies, which I began applying to my leadership role and all of the speaking engagements I had at the time. Ultimately it became clear that I had begun a journey that would significantly impact my worldview.

This newfound understanding of how missiology could help a busy mission leader like me was that it gave me a lens—or at times a set of lenses—through which to look at the world from the viewpoint of commitment to the Christian faith.

Over time I have discovered dozens of mission leaders who have also felt that something was missing in their leadership. Just like me, these leaders were focused on plans, strategies, budgets and of course results. Many have felt they had no voice with the church, Bible colleges and seminaries, mission leaders, and missiologists. They were under pressure to find their own leadership voice and influence.

I have learnt that leaders are good at being practitioners because we want to be people of action. However in doing so we might lack reflection, unknowingly missing the combined benefits. We need both—we should be reflective-practitioners.

When faced with his new leadership appointment, King Solomon was given the choice to ask for anything he wanted. He prayed for wisdom to discern the times, so that he would know what to do (1 Kings 3). This has often been my prayer—Lord, help me to be reflective so that I know how to act as I seek the holistic transformation of the people and communities I serve.

## Addressing the 'Why' Before the 'What'

The significance of this chapter for leadership in community lies in recognizing the contribution that reflective practitioners make to the *missio Dei*. Reflection makes a re-balancing of one's practice possible. In missional terminology, withdrawing to reflect enables a greater engagement with one's context, because it creates space for the quietness of the Holy Spirit to speak, to direct, and to bring wisdom.

Before describing what it means to be a reflective practitioner, or outlining what is referred to as the consultative process, understand that this chapter is not intended to create or promote a prescribed, teachable methodology for becoming a reflective practitioner—a sort of 'add-on' or goal that leaders can embrace. Ideally, leadership seeks to develop a culture of reflectivity, where missional leaders see reflection informing action as a natural habit, allowing for discernment in community.

Encouraging current and emerging WGA leaders to value becoming reflective practitioners, and to engage with a consultative process, has been a complex and creative venture. Drawing from experiences leading the WGA, allow me to illustrate this further.

WGA began to develop its own missiological expertise as early as 2006 when, originally, none existed. Over time, WGA's missiological consultative process has gathered practitioners and theorists from across the globe. They have reflected together on the *missio Dei* and its practical benefits for Bible translation movements.

WGA leaders are continually learning how to create frameworks to identify and discuss relevant missiological topics. In order for mission theory to remain relevant and contribute to current issues affecting practice, theorists and practitioners need to identify important topics for missiological study and reflection. Giving time for reflection allows opportunity to consider topics needing examination in mission today.

Missiological reflection is best done in a multi- and inter-cultural community because this enables collective listening to the Holy Spirit. The process of discernment is the critical step in missional thinking.[1] Emerging reflective practitioners have shaped WGA's leadership culture in such a way that leaders are equipped to think, discuss and strategize through sound missiological understanding.

WGA's missiological consultative process has enabled a growing body of globally minded leaders to think and act missionally and lead more effectively within the changing contexts of the church and world.

Why is this recounting of the recent WGA leadership journey relevant to missional leadership in community, especially in the Western church?

One strong reason is recognizing that the church of the global South and East is actively initiating its own plans for integral mission—the proclamation and demonstration of the gospel. This may be problematic for the Western church because of its difficulty in listening well to the rest of the world. Particularly notable is Western-centric scholarship in theological reflection. Western missions are closely tied to their culture, which is noted for its political and economic pragmatism. The results are a growing gap between Western mission practice and global South and East interpretation of mission.

A challenge facing mission theorists is how to collaborate with practitioners and theorists from the global South and East. Western missiological-theological discussions emphasize the theoretical over the experiential.[2] The consequence is that global South and East experiences are often undervalued from a missional perspective.

Instead of trying to propose some manner of missional counter-balance, let's remember that missional leadership relies on the inner transformation of the leader first. This, in turn, leads to the release of an innovative spiritual gift of leadership to lead and equip the transformation of God's people so they may effectively participate in God's mission in their particular contexts. And *that* is the starting point for the proper valuing of each other's perspectives—whether our Christian heritage is from the North, South, East or West.

Simply put, the process of missional leadership becoming reflective practitioners is an important contribution to the effectiveness of global, missional leadership in community.

## The Reflective Practitioner

A major influence on my own leadership journey occurred in 2006 when William (Bill) Taylor was invited to facilitate a missiological consultation for selected leaders in Wycliffe Bible Translators International—later to become the Wycliffe Global Alliance.

Taylor introduced the concept of a reflective practitioner—a new concept for all the participants. His use of the term originated from the 1999 World Evangelical Alliance Iguassu Missiological Consultation. He defines the reflective practitioner as 'women and men of both action and study; rooted in the Word of God and the church of Christ; passionately obedient to the fullness of the Great Commandment and Great Commission; globalized in their perspective; yet faithful citizens of their own cultures'.[3] Such people, he suggests, cover the spectrum from younger to older, more or less experienced, 'who combine body and mind in their passion for God and his world'.[4]

According to Taylor's definition, the reflective practitioner displays certain fundamental characteristics. This person anchors his or her action and study upon the Bible, has an awareness of global realities and the church, and understands how to integrate these components into their response to God's invitation to join him in his mission. The reflective practitioner's goal is to demonstrate an integrated nature—action and study that is glocal and global, Christ-centred and biblical.

**Characteristics of a Reflective Practitioner**

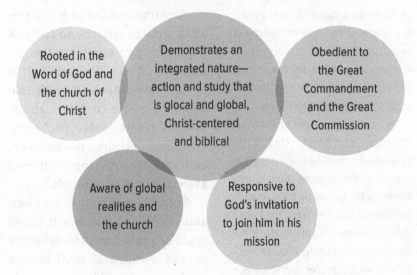

At this point, readers may assume a need to make time for such reflection, and to suspect that there may be a hint of daydreaming involved. These would be correct observations on both counts.

Long time friend and colleague on the WGA leadership team, Susan Van Wynen, notes that in essence, the reflective practitioner uses a 'reflective lens' to critically analyse practice, and creates the time and space that enables reflectivity, so that new ideas may emerge.[5] This is a

## My Journey as a Reflective Practitioner

*by Minyoung Jung*

Something big was missing. Ever since I started getting involved in Christian ministries four decades ago—including campus evangelism, local churches and eventually missions—I had constantly felt emptiness, as if something substantial was absent. Regardless of the type of ministry or organization, Christian workers in general were expected to push themselves as hard as possible to achieve the prescribed (thus unchallenged) goals.

In retrospect, it's not just a Western issue. The Korean church has been greatly indebted to the sacrificial service of the Western church, and inevitably influenced by them, in both positive and negative ways. But I don't think the Korean church can blame the Western church blindly, since task-orientation without proper time and space for reflection is coming from the global wave of industrialization on the one hand, and more fundamentally from sinful human nature on the other. The case of the church in Ephesus in Revelation 2 (which was of the East rather than the West) may be a relevant example.

discipline. It may even look a little like daydreaming, which is simply turning one's thoughts from the present, and does not have to be frivolous. For some, 'creating space' to reflect and consider involves movement, e.g. taking a walk, or listening to music. But the key aspect is the discipline of decidedly making the time to both refresh one's thoughts on a topic, and to apply critical thinking to it.

According to David Rock, creating time to reflect and to think happens when one takes the initiative, and is 'self-directed'. It is in such times, Rock observes, that people are able to 'learn, think, invent, create, solve problems, visualize, rethink, re-engineer', and so forth, making their own associations in their minds.[6]

Socrates' maxim that the unexamined life is not worth living could be applied to a non-reflective person who, because of human weaknesses, could become a problem to those around him or her. Having courage to deal with personal difficulties is a critical trait, because it enables a person to overcome adversity by standing firm for what they believe, admitting their mistakes and successfully battling inner turmoil or external opposition.[7]

In other words, reflection facilitates examination.

While one needs to 'retreat and reflect', one must also 'engage and act'.[8] Mark Sayers proposes a process of 'withdrawal-return' so that a leader gets 'critical distance [from] the myths and illusions' of one's culture in order to 'break their spell'. Once balance is re-gained, the leader returns refreshed and ready to lead again.[9]

Leaders who are reflective practitioners also need to be lifelong learners who are growing in 'self-knowledge and awareness' because they are committed to continually studying local-regional-global contexts in order to identify opportunities and challenges.[10] Roxburgh and Romanuk identify two interconnected skills that are needed: (1) asking new kinds of questions that bring insights 'beneath the surface... to deeper levels of meaning'; and (2) letting the biblical narratives 'ask their own questions' of the context.[11]

This all sounds like a tall order. In my own experience with the WGA, the revelation of the

God acknowledged their hard work and perseverance in the midst of hardships, yet reproved them for forsaking their first love. Then God commanded them to reflect on the height from which they had fallen and to repent and do the things they did at first.

In 2006, my role in the Wycliffe Global Alliance's reflective and consultative journey came as a timely rescue. I had almost given up Christian ministry because of burnout. The spiritual emptiness caused by constantly pushing myself harder made me yearn for and welcome this major shift in what I had experienced in prior Wycliffe corporate culture, as well as my Korean culture. And, in turn, the reflective consultative process has served as a diagnosis of, and a remedy for, my emptiness, that 'something big' that had been lacking. For the past ten years, consequently, I have been an avid follower, advocate and promoter of this meaningful journey within and outside of WGA. I have made conscious efforts to be a reflective leader, colleague, speaker, networker, etc., encouraging and facilitating reflective learning communities to be formed within the variety of Christian networks where I was involved.

A reflective practice is not just adding one more burdensome action called reflection to already overloaded shoulders. It is a different way of carrying out our responsibilities, a healthy way of participating in God's mission by integrating our tasks with sound biblical principles. We should remember that even though the Israelites were zealous for God, their zeal was not based on true knowledge, which I believe can be attained only through reflection. Therefore, not knowing the righteousness that comes from God, they sought to establish their own (Romans 10:2-3). Doing missions without constant reflection is not only ineffective but also often counterproductive. Applying this to the church in Ephesus, reflective practice is about doing the hard work while energized by the first love. It is about spreading the love of God to the world by being constantly supplied with His love by His Spirit (Romans 5:5). It is about us, the branches, being engrafted to Christ, the true vine, to be able to bear healthy fruit. It is about a Christian community, whether it be a local church, mission agency or alliance becoming a 'missional being' for doing missions.

Being reflective is contagious. Since a sustained reflective process changes one's perspective and attitude significantly, it inevitably affects people within one's influence-sphere. My responsibility as a facilitator of church engagement and networking gave me the privilege of connections and interactions with various global churches and mission movements. After an initial proactive investment in some strategic networks and relationships with key leaders, I have been steadily invited to various collaborating opportunities without exerting my own initiative, proving that many Christian workers and leaders out there feel the same emptiness and thirst I used to feel in 'doing missions' without proper reflection.

Reflective practice has liberated me from unhealthy competition and inordinate pressure for quick results to prove myself, enabling me to pursue genuine Kingdom partnerships. Reflective practitioners are non-threatening to Christian colleagues, coming to the partnership roundtable without hidden agendas, seeking to edify the Kingdom of God rather than pursuing individual goals. Reflective practitioners are the ones needed for this new era of 'the global mission by the global church'.

importance of developing leaders as reflective practitioners is not radical *per se*, since the concept of reflective practice is not new to missiology, theology or social sciences.

But what has made all the difference is detailed in the next section: linking the growth of reflective practitioners with well-designed consultative processes wherein individual leaders engage in, and model, leadership in community.

# Using a Missiological Consultative Process

The single greatest discovery of the WGA missiological consultative process has been the importance of missional leaders becoming reflective practitioners.

In the broadest sense, what is a missiological consultative process? And can an examination of this process uncover deeper meanings of issues facing leaders and their organizations?

'Missiological consultative process' may sound complex, even convoluted. But in the end it is not so much what the process is called, but that it is encouraged to happen—to grow—even in organic ways.

And grow where?

From my own observations, mission agency and church leadership attuned to the mission of God can find extensive value in allowing space for meaningful times of reflection, discussion and collective listening within a consultative framework. This viewpoint is not intended to challenge existing strategic planning methodologies employed by leaders and organizations, but rather to shine a light on processes aimed at leaders co-discovering and articulating underlying values that drive organizational goals—especially in light of changing global contexts.

As indicated in the book's subtitle, this is a journey, and the missiological consultative process is the mode of transport that takes you on this journey.

Stephen Coertze is the resident missiologist for WGA. Over the years, I have called upon him not only to lead various consultations, but also to help describe the process.

Coertze states that a missiological consultation is when missiologists use their knowledge, skills and understandings of the academic field of missiology to assist others (groups or individuals) through a consultative process, to understand or evaluate a certain topic pertaining to the group.

Such a consultative process can be conducted in a variety of ways. Among others, it can be done through facilitation or participation in a discussion with an intended purpose and outcome. It can also be done through research and the write-up of the research findings that will then be presented to the parties involved.[12]

The purpose of a consultation will differ depending on the topic to be explored. It could be as basic as ensuring that the topic is explored from a biblical foundation. It could involve an evaluation of a set of practices, philosophies or policies. Or it could even help set direction for the organization or group.[13]

The nature of a missiological consultative process may raise pertinent issues to be addressed, or it could stimulate broader reflection on issues than what might normally take place.

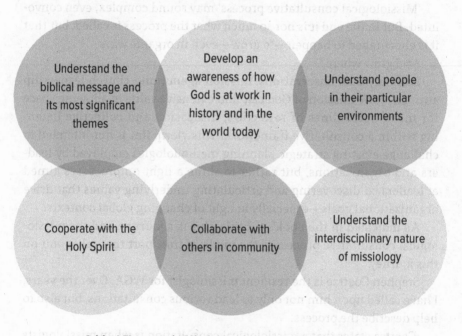

**Critical Elements in Missiology for a Consultative Process**

According to Coertze's observations, there are a number of critical elements in missiology that should feature simultaneously in a consultative process. Some of these are:

- understand the biblical message and its most significant themes;
- develop an awareness of how God is at work in history and in the world today;

- understand people in their particular environments;
- cooperate with the Holy Spirit;
- collaborate with others in community; and
- understand the interdisciplinary nature of missiology.[14]

Other factors of importance in creating a missiological consultative process are the composition of the group (who participates and why), the number of participants (smaller numbers may bring greater depth to discussions), the geographic location (an unfamiliar scene may bring greater insights), how the main topic will be developed and discussed, and how the consultation will be facilitated (to ensure that appropriate adult-learning techniques are employed).[15]

It is interesting to note that in 2007, I collated some recommendations from the participants attending the second WGA missiological consultation, convened in Singapore. I believe the recommendations largely ring as true and helpful today as then. I'll paraphrase a few that stand out:

1. Develop a core group of missiological 'reflectors' within the leadership, who can then:
   - facilitate missiological reflection across the organization, or church, or network of partnering agencies far beyond the scope limited to occasional consultations;
   - help the organization or church or network engage at the global level to influence missiological dialogue and strategy; and
   - assist both existing and emerging leaders who prefer to be pragmatic to instead articulate their agency's purpose in terms of the global context of the mission of God.
2. Intentionally develop a community of reflective practitioners: One benefit of this would be the contribution toward longer-term transformations, rather than demonstrating an interest only in shorter-term goals associated with efficiency.
3. Consider formal training in missiology: Some leaders would benefit from graduate or post-graduate studies in missiology. Financial assistance for study programs should be encouraged.

4. Promote culture shift through reflection and the consultative processes: This would help mission agencies, partnering networks and churches become missional *in essence*—without having to make missiology an institutional department.

In terms of missional leadership, there will inevitably be times of some form of agency identity crisis, or mission drift—especially as leadership faces challenges in responding to issues stemming from, among other things, globalization. Here is the overarching realization: the habit and practice of discovering—or re-discovering—foundational group values via reflective/consultative processes allows for a continuous influx of the Holy Spirit in a world full of discontinuous change.

And, importantly, this involves the spiritual and natural maturity of each participant engaged in a group's reflective/consultative process. It involves experience in a particular multi-dimensional way of critical thinking. It involves global connectedness and thinking. It involves a good measure of illumination and wisdom that God, through His Spirit and presence, gives to a group that no cognitive brilliance of any group can provide on its own.

# Questions for Consideration and Discussion

1. After reading this chapter, how might you (ideally in conversation with your small group or team) identify factors in your church, ministry or other organization, that either hinder or promote being a reflective-practitioner?

2. Within the context of your small group or team, consider examples from mission agencies or churches (including your own), where 'collective listening' to the Holy Spirit was demonstrated in ministry planning or strategy sessions.

3. Can you envision how a missiological consultative process might be developed and applied in your context? Discuss in your small group or team why you'd consider it to be of value.

1. After reading this chapter, how might you (ideally in conversation with your small group or team) identify factors in your edition, ministry or other organization, that either hinder or promote being a reflective practitioner?

# Generosity in Spirit and Practice
# in the *Missio Dei*

I am to be a steward of all that God has entrusted to me, since everything comes from God in the first place. Therefore, generosity should be a basic characteristic of my life, and for all Christians. The Apostle Paul affirms this point in Romans 11:36: 'For from him and through him and for him are all things. To him be the glory forever! Amen.' We know that God's love and generosity are without limits (John 3:16, 17). Stewardship is interconnected with generosity. We need to be generous with each other because God has been generous with us. To personalize this, I am called by God to be generous as I fulfil his mandate for me to be a steward of his creation.

As part of the 2016 Wycliffe Global Gathering in Thailand, our facilitation team led a process called the 'Third Table Community Experience', with the focus on strengthening healthy biblical communities in the Alliance. The 150+ participants were seated in groups associated with these five regions of the world: Africa, Asia, Canada/USA, Europe, and Latin America/Caribbean. They were asked to identify characteristic beliefs, values, attitudes or practices from their regions that they could offer as gifts to the rest of the Alliance to build healthy biblical communities. A total of 15 gifts were offered. Then, each region identified which of the gifts they were ready to receive.

One of the gifts was titled 'Hospitality and Generosity: We are generous with our time, energy and resources; caring, friendly, sacrificial in giving.' Each region responded differently to this gift. For example, Latin America/Caribbean stated, 'Yes, we believe that being part of the Alliance is not just being friends but sharing what we have with others.' Europe stated that they were 'ready to receive, but know it will be difficult. We want to receive it because it's a biblical concept. Our culture and the Bible recommend this gift of generosity. We want to aim for this but are not there yet (especially sacrificial giving).' Indonesians in the Asia group responded, 'The desire comes from our group to put this as a value. We desire to build community. We desire to build relationship/friendship.' The African delegation stated, 'We agree, because we value people before all. Resources are secondary.' The US and Canada said 'We need to be able to give and receive. God gives us resources and we must be willing to give those resources to benefit the community.'

This process highlights the importance of developing an intentional acceptance of generosity as we participate together in God's mission.

At another session in the same Global Gathering, our leaders hosted a discussion about generosity in funding with a focus on the need to see greater financial generosity from all parts of the world in order to meet needs in Bible translation movements. Participants shared their insights and observations. A Pacific Islander stated, 'Our financial generosity is matched by dollars in the North. But we see generosity in all we give: friendship, time, etc. Sometimes it is hard to relate to rich donors. It makes it difficult for us to be actively involved in the work.'

This brings to light the inherent tensions we encounter when we partner together in mission. We need grace towards each other as we navigate through the complexity of stewardship and generosity in a global community.

## What is the 'Coin of the Realm' in God's Kingdom?

One understanding of the phrase 'coin of the realm' is something valued or used as if it were the official currency of a nation.[1] Taken in this sense, and relating it to God's kingdom—or more to the point, God's mission—what is of value that is used as a form of exchange among church and global mission partners? Perhaps the better but tougher question is: what *should* this be?

If leadership in organizations cannot process and address these questions, or worse, cannot acknowledge them, then there is considerable risk of tainting multiple layers of ministry plans, as well as the community of relationships involved.

One of the greatest challenges in partnering in mission is how money is used. In most mission partnerships, one group will inevitably have more financial resources than the other. When the rich let go of 'the burden of wealth', there must be open and honest discussions with all involved in order to prevent dependency or paternalism.[2]

The general use (or misuse) of power in mission is integrated with money and funding. Underlying Alex Araujo and Werner Mischke's models of power-based control are the metaphors of two types of boats. The 'powerboat' is characterized by high-control, self-reliance and a dependence on efficiency through Western technology and management methodology. The 'sailboat', with its shared-control, relies on the 'wind' of the Holy Spirit who works in the affairs of God's kingdom and is the 'force' that enables and guides God's mission. When it comes to fundraising and relating to donors, the powerboat metaphor applies, in particular, when larger amounts of funds are involved, or come from Western sources.[3] The implication is that speed and efficiency are more important than relationships, community and generosity. In contrast, the sailboat model gives intentional space for the strengthening of friendship leading to greater collaboration, partnership and generosity, because the value of each of the partners is recognized and affirmed.

## Models of Power-based Control

| Powerboat | Sailboat |
|---|---|
| High-control, self-reliance, dependence on efficiency through Western technology and management methodology | Shared-control, relies on the 'wind' of the Holy Spirit—the 'force' that enables and guides God's mission |

These factors of Western missionary wealth and dependency may affect mission movements and churches in the global South. They may be unable to be self-supporting and self-governing because the control of financial resources may still be influenced by the paternalism of Western mission partnerships, or Western reliance upon expensive strategies. In addition, the expectations of greater accountability, influenced by Western business marketing, may lead to greater misunderstandings in global South contexts as to why these expectations exist.[4] Left unchecked, the 'power of money readily sets the agenda' for mission.[5]

## The rise of the donor-philanthropist

Gilles Gravelle describes modern philanthropists who want to fund mission: 'Much of their wealth was generated by new ideas that took hold, so they seek involvement in projects that apply new, innovative ways of doing things. They are not interested in an agency's traditions or status quo thinking, if those things prevent the development of creative solutions to today's problems.'[6]

Today's donor-philanthropist doesn't just want to invest funds in mission but also wants to invest ideas and time. Reporting back to the donor is critically important too. However, the donor wants to know the whole story, including problems and failures of the ministry projects being supported, because these are important issues to monitor. Today's donor-philanthropist is suspicious of 'impact reports that only focus on positive outcomes... because they know that in the real world things rarely go perfectly according to plan'.[7]

Donors today are known to be bypassing Western mission structures in order to give directly to indigenous ministries in the majority world. They are concerned about the rising costs associated with internal operating budgets of institutional mission agencies, and wonder if these structures are actually important to the achievement of mission goals.

## From charity to partnership—the language of giving

Gravelle further notes the changing language of giving through the ages: (1) In the 18th century: *Charity* (Christian love and therefore giving to needy causes was a good way for Christians to show love); (2) In the 19th century: *Benevolence* (giving as an act of good will or kindness; also for some, a synonym for funding the churches' programs); (3) In the 20th century: *Stewardship* (givers took more personal spiritual responsibility in managing the money that God had entrusted to them for the benefit of others; this also brought performance benchmarks and other accountability practices associated with grants); and (4) In the 21st century: *Partnership* (givers are increasingly dissatisfied with giving through an agency and they don't want to be separated as donor from the recipient).[8]

Today's donor uses language from the business world such as the following:

1. *Investment*: What you are sacrificially providing to launch and grow the ministry effort;
2. *Business model*: Steps to accomplish your visionary goals;
3. *Performance*: How progress is made to accomplish the goals;
4. *Return on investment (ROI)*: Good effects of the project based on what it cost to achieve it;
5. *Measurement metrics*: The sorts of things that confirm the mission goals are being achieved;
6. *Scorecard*: Comparison of mission statement to what is actually being accomplished by the mission work; and
7. *Annual yield*: Good results over the year.[9]

Indeed, many mission agencies produce annual reports and other communication pieces that reflect modern business language as applied to ministry goals, and are still adjusting to the rise and influence of the modern donor-philanthropist. Some agencies have bought fully into the notion that the donor-philanthropist has the ultimate power and influence in mission today. Others are not so sure.

## Further tensions

The intrinsic tension between themes of wealth and power, poverty and disempowerment is another reason why the topic of money in mission is not a neutral concept. McGlory Speckman detects the intertwined relationship between power and wealth and how accruing wealth leads to a position of power.[10] Either power determines one's wealth, or wealth places a person in a powerful position. Bonk submits that wealth and power create challenges in mission because Christianity was not intended to make people content with power and wealth. He suggests that widespread wealth has 'never been the norm of human experience'. Instead, survival and 'subsistence' has been typical for most pre-industrial age societies.[11] This observation may get lost today because of economic globalization. Nonetheless, it is a factor when considering funding God's mission due to large parts of the world still being in the grip of abject poverty.

## Divine generosity: no PIN or password required

Kelly Kapic observes that there is a 'divine generosity' expressed in the gospel that includes God's love, righteousness, hope and work of grace.[12] Accepting these gifts means entering into God's lavish life. R. Scott Rodin defines 'Christ-centred generosity [as] the nature of one's heart that is rich toward God'. This is a primary characteristic of 'an obedient and joyful steward'.[13] Dennis Tongoi calls generosity 'a reflection of the freedom' that arises from being a Christian.[14]

Believing in God means believing in his 'blessed community', the church, and joining God's 'movement of divine generosity'.[15] Tongoi claims that everybody can live a generous life. It is not dependent upon what kind of resources they own or manage.[16] Zenet Maramara calls generosity an 'overflow of the steward's grateful response to God' because of God's daily generosity to his people.[17] Living generously, as Kapic proposes, includes how finances are managed, but most of all it is a holistic vision because it includes how one loves people across all barriers, whether they be geographical, religious, educational, political or racial.[18]

## Issues of dependency

Dependency, according to Robert Reese, originated with colonial era practices of financial subsidies from foreign missionaries who gave money to local pastors and evangelists.[19] It may continue today through missionary paternalism, whether expressed in short-term mission teams seeking to do good (but sometimes on their own terms), or from partnerships between dominating Western organizations, mission agencies and churches in association with those from the global South and East. Reese notes the shift that often takes place in these partnerships, when dependency on various kinds of material and technological resources replaces the gospel and new life in Christ.[20]

Bonk claims that the Western missionary movement and the accompanying Western prosperity are being challenged by ethical and theological predicaments caused by its own affluence.[21] Consequently, Western missionaries may be associated with the wealth of their nations, so it is no surprise that biblical admonition on the subject of the poor and wealthy 'makes very uncomfortable reading'. It follows that those who 'live privileged lives among the poor' find it difficult to teach about generosity.[22]

# Principles—not Prescriptions

Though rarely straightforward, the matter of raising and managing funds affects how global missional structures function and are led, and is of on-going interest and concern.

Managing financial resources not only affects the praxis of global mission leadership, but it is also based upon a Trinitarian theology of self-sacrifice and giving, since God is generous and wisely provides from his own resources.[23] Unless this sensitive topic of funding God's mission is released from its Western cultural boundaries and influences, it will continue to contribute undue influence over leaders of all nationalities and levels of responsibility.

# Transformative Generosity

*by José de Dios*

In my work with *Generosity Path* (a global movement to encourage biblical generosity), I have been talking to people from different walks of life about the concept of generosity. These discussions are not a ploy to get money from them, or to have them join a specific cause. Rather, as a facilitator of intentional conversations about this issue, I'm always seeking to understand people's journey of generosity.

As we talk about the timeless values and practices of generosity found throughout Scripture, to my surprise, people often share with me their own stories of generosity. From social causes to personal experiences a theme emerges: those who live out the concept of generosity are deeply transformed by it. Yes, they help others. They become part of wider, lasting change. They impact their communities, their countries and their families. 'The Cause' is still important to them. But few of them start out realizing just how much

## A wealth of generosity and funding resources

The themes of generosity in mission, stewardship of God's resources, accountability, ethical considerations and other related topics are growing. Entire networks have been created to provide training, educational resources, conferences and other tools. Taking a lead in this regard is the Global Generosity Network—an initiative of the World Evangelical Alliance.

Another important resource is the *Lausanne Standards,* which began as an outgrowth of discussions by an assembly of Western and global South and East leaders in November 2006, at an event held by the Lausanne Movement at the Oxford Centre for Mission Studies. This resulted in a task force developing standards for international funding partnerships and relationships, with an ongoing aim to provide guidance for further dialogue between Western funders and global South and East ministry partners.

## Developing funding principles

Drawing from my own experience leading the WGA, the matter of funding Bible translation movements provided a learning opportunity at a global level. One reason for this was the recognition that WGA is comprised of a mixture of what might be called legacy Wycliffe organizations from nations with extensive histories using working funding methodologies, and a variety of often smaller organizations from the global South and East with similar vision for Bible translation—but differing perspectives especially on local expressions of funding translation projects.

In 2012, I asked Stephen Coertze to begin developing a process for a series of five missiological consultations to be convened on the topic of 'Funding God's Mission'. As a result, he produced a framework with two purposes: (1) to increase 'individual and collective missiological understanding of the participants' about funding; and (2) to communicate a renewed 'vision for funding practices for God's mission' established by a set of guiding principles.[24]

generosity will change them.

Thinking of others, being part of something bigger than themselves takes their focus off themselves. Whatever challenges they are facing, whatever worries plague their work, suddenly appear smaller, more manageable, in the face of the good they are able to effect. Some would claim this type of generosity is ultimately self-serving: I give because it makes me feel good, and a little less guilty for having so much. Perhaps. Human nature is funny that way. But the people I've spoken with were sincerely generous, happier, and in turn, even more generous because of what they have witnessed.

Another theme that emerges is: no matter how much you have, or how much you give, you can *live* generosity. This is important in the context of a global community, where some have much and others have less. It counteracts the subtle message that only those who have lots of resources can effectively accomplish the Great Commission.

Giving generously can take many forms, but there's something about giving money that seems to make a significant difference to the one who gives. People give time, they give information or ideas, and all those are needed. However, when someone gives money, it's as if it releases some unseen transformative power, both for the giver and for the receiver. This is not to suggest that there's a hierarchy of giving, with money at the top. Rather, because money is so vital to our survival in today's world, sharing with others is transformative.

Speaking pragmatically, money is needed to effect real change, to live with dignity and provide for loved ones. And there is sacredness in taking one of our most valuable assets, which we probably worked very hard to attain, and sharing it with others. This doesn't negate the genuine risks of giving money carelessly or unwisely. However, when we invest our finances to help others lift themselves with dignity out of a difficult reality we are living authentically.

What I find most encouraging is recognizing the desire of missional communities, agencies and leaders to live out this life of generosity together. At the heart of it is seeing the giving and receiving of gifts (financial and otherwise) as part of *missio Dei*, and not simply as means to achieve the ends of a particular cause or institution. It is acknowledging and seeking solutions to how a perceived difference in power can deeply impact partnership and collaboration, both for those who have more finances, and those with less. This could have a profoundly transformational effect on relationships, and on the long-term success, not only of our work together but also of our testimony to the world.

A generous community is sensitive to the needs of others, connected in deep relationships where we seek to bless one another, not just 'help' those who have less. It restores dignity where dependence and paternalism have become rooted. It recognizes that each person, and each community, has been called to participate in God's Mission, and is uniquely gifted by the Creator to play a role in it. Generous communities recognize that all that we possess is entrusted to us in order to fulfil God's purpose on the Earth, to 'proclaim freedom for the prisoners, and recovery of sight for the blind, to set the oppressed free, to proclaim the year of the Lord's favor' (Luke 4:18-19).

The principles were to be 'missiologically sound, contextually relevant, sustainable [and] globally respectful'. Each consultation would therefore 'identify... existing funding practices and the beliefs and values that underlie them, [and] explore missiologically sound guiding principles on funding'.[25]

The five consultations consisted of an initial gathering in 2013 with a global representation of leaders, to be followed up with four regional events in 2014. Those four locations were Thailand, Germany, Kenya and Mexico. Attendance at the regional forums was comprised of leaders of WGA organizations from their respective areas.

## Summarizing the initial global consultation

The first missiological consultation on 'Funding God's Mission' was held in Turkey. The 36 participants from 19 nations represented a diverse grouping of global contexts with the majority holding senior leadership level positions in their mission and church organizations.

In their feedback, some relevant themes emerged, including: (1) the desire for a sensitive and responsive environment within missional communities that will accept the reality of multiple cultures and contexts functioning together; (2) the request for space and opportunities for the church of the global South and East to give an influential voice in funding policies and practices within mission communities; (3) the desire to have systems that resource missional ministry that are built upon the dignity and community of participants; and (4) the aspiration for accountability processes that are contextually sensitive, respectful of all missional partners, and that build relationships of trust.

At the conclusion of this first in a series of five consultations, Minyoung Jung gave this summary: This was not a problem-solving workshop but a reflective consultation. It is a journey, which has only started. There is a call for a 'biblically sound and practically sustainable funding system', which must not dehumanize the recipient(s). We are developing guiding principles rather than funding models (which may come later). There is an inherent danger in 'benchmarking specific models that have been influenced by... historical factors [such] as colonialism, rationalism, individualism, triumphalism, racism and sexism'. Funding 'global mission may require a fundamentally different approach' than just modifying the established paradigm. 'God's mission does not depend upon our own ability or our resources.'[26]

Each of the four subsequent regional consultations held discussions based on the same framework as the global consultation, and produced their own summaries.

Some months after the final regional event, an editorial team synthesized the input from all of the consultations into a short document titled:

# The WGA Principles for Funding

### Principles 1-4: God's mission belongs to him:

1. The mission of God is fulfilled by the Father, Son and Holy Spirit in perfect unity.
2. Everything belongs to God, including all the resources necessary to fulfil his mission.
3. God invites and enables his global Church to creatively participate with him in his mission.
4. God's love and generosity are without limits.

### Principles 5-7: God provides for his mission:

5. God creatively provides for his mission through a diversity of people, means and resources.
6. As God's image bearers, and following his example, each person can joyfully and generously give according to the blessings God has given.
7. Recognising God's intention for provision through community, the sharing of God's gifts and resources, including money, is encouraged so that all may benefit.

### Principles 8-14: God enables us to share his resources:

8. All that we have is from God.
9. Participating in the funding of God's mission is an act of worship.
10. We give from what God has given us, acknowledging our dependence on him through prayer and obedience.
11. No individual or group is self-sufficient. Sharing resources is an interdependent relational activity where all people and their contributions are valued and every person can graciously give and receive.

12. The sharing of resources needs to be sensitive and responsive to multiple cultures and contexts.

13. In the process of giving and receiving, the dignity of all is honoured and valued through respectful relationships and friendships.

14. When plans among funding partners work out differently than expected, it is an opportunity to come together in an atmosphere of grace to discern and align with what God is doing.

**Principles 15-19: God expects wise stewardship of his resources:**

15. Stewardship and accountability are important to God, therefore we are mutually responsible to use his resources ethically and wisely.

16. Stewardship values are developed and tested within community according to biblical principles.

17. A collective understanding of funding needs is determined through consideration of many factors, including missiological and theological reflection and dialogue.

18. Transparent communication and trusting relationships are essential for dialogue regarding needs, and for avoiding issues concerning power, pride and control.

19. Discernment in funding decisions includes prayer, reflection, [the inclusion of] diverse voices and recognition of God's mission and his focus on the transformation and holistic restoration of people.

## Observations about the *Principles for Funding*

The entire undertaking of establishing the *Principles for Funding* spanned 18 months and involved 145 people from 51 nations. This level of participation from such a diversity of nations gives reason to present the process of developing these principles here, as it provided a wide-ranging level of engagement on the topic of funding God's mission—well beyond just the context of funding Bible translation movements.

The participants discussed the changing contexts of global and local funding in light of biblical principles. This gave an environment to develop 'relationships, listen to diverse voices, gain insights and discern together opportunities and responsibilities regarding funding as a part of God's mission'.[27]

The WGA *Principles for Funding* are not implementation protocols or best practices guidelines. They are values-driven and start from the basis of acknowledging that God's mission belongs to him.

This underlying recognition can serve as a continuing levelling influence for church and mission agency leadership grappling with issues surrounding funding—whether glocal or global—and additionally point to the overarching theme of generosity in spirit and in practice.

···  ···

# Questions for Consideration and Discussion

1. In the opening story of this chapter, a point is made about '... the importance of developing an intentional acceptance of generosity...'. In your small group or team, discuss what this looks like (or might look like) in the context of a church or agency ministry partnership familiar to you. Consider the perspective of the intended recipient of an act of generosity; describe what you think it might mean (for them) to accept such generosity.

2. Discuss with others in your small group what insights you gained considering the powerboat and the sailboat as metaphors in relation to issues concerning funds, power and influence in ministry.

3. Pick one or two of the *Principles for Funding* as presented in the chapter and discuss in your small group or team how they might be considered by leadership of a church or organization you're a part of—especially those leaders involved in the raising and managing of funds. Then discuss how those principles may affect your own understanding of generosity in spirit and in practice.

## Questions for Consideration and Discussion

1. In the opening story of this chapter, a point is made about ... the importance of developing an intentional acceptance of generosity ... In your small group or team, discuss what this looks like for (might look like) in the context of a church or agency ministry partnership familiar to you. Consider the perspective of the intended recipient of such generosity; describe what you think it might mean (for them) to accept such generosity.

# Third Way Thinking in the *Missio Dei*

I was born and raised in Papua New Guinea (PNG), but my parents came from the US. Because of this, I proudly identify myself as a 'Third Culture Kid', or TCK. My parents were missionary Bible translators amongst the Kewa speaking people of PNG. When I was three months old they took me into the village of Muli, where I grew up speaking Kewa as my first language. When my parents spoke to me in English, I replied in Kewa. Manoa, the chief, once said to us, 'When you first came, your skin was white, ours was black and we were different on the inside. Now your skin is still white and our skin is still black, but we are the same on the inside, because you speak our language.'

Every four years or so, my parents took me back to the US to visit friends, supporters and relatives. My father studied in Australia, so we lived there twice. We also lived for a time in New Zealand. Therefore, as a boy, I was regularly going back and forth between different countries and cultures. But throughout my life I held to and identified with my PNG roots. Part of my identity is still Papua New Guinean, and I am reminded of this every time I return there. During a recent visit, a PNG leader stated without hesitation that I was 'one of their sons'.

Being a TCK gives me a great sense of responsibility to use the perspectives I gained in my upbringing to address areas that hold us back in God's mission. For example, God created all people in his image (Genesis 1:26), and yet we are all very different from each other, speaking different languages, having differing cultures, and living with various world views. How do we transcend these factors to find ways of working together that honour the Lord and fulfil his vision for us to 'be one' (John 17:21)?

This is where the point of view of a TCK can be helpful. TCK's learn how to navigate between many different cultures while often feeling at home in each one.

TCKs can provide insights into third-way thinking, finding innovative methods of creating third spaces between very different groups of people, settings, environments and so forth. Developing third spaces enables us to live out values of the kingdom of God as members of Christ's body. Each part of the body is needed, and our role has been to ensure that the body is healthy, growing, and effective.

As leaders in God's mission we have an important role to play in discerning when and how to create new third spaces. In this regard, I borrow from the insights of Andrew Walls who observes a tradition of the New Zealand Maoris who 'speak of the future as being behind us. We cannot see it. The past is what is in front of us. We can see that stretched out before us, the most recent plainly, the more distant shading away to the horizon.'[1] In other words, we can't predict what third spaces may need to be created in God's mission. However, what we can do is to follow Walls' advice and 'look at the past in front of us and see what it suggests of the way that we have come and perhaps read in outline, as on a sketch map, the place to which we have been brought now'.[2] This implies a willingness to adapt and incorporate new, third ways of thinking, as the Holy Spirit leads us.

# Are There New Ways for Navigating and Working in God's Mission?

The answer to the above question sets up a key issue explored in this chapter—that of using a binary choice. Often my own almost unconscious default is to apply binary logic, presuming that the answer is either 'yes' or 'no', or perhaps yes or no, with caveats. And while making choices—anything from which soap product to use, to planning mission agency strategy—often involves a 'this or that' style of determination, there are different perspectives to employ.

A challenge for mission agencies and the church is to address the suggestion that organizational leadership structures are 'at least 50 years old [and] stuck in the Industrial Era'.[3] This affects mission relationships, partnerships, and how discussions and decisions are made. Increasingly needed are third ways of thinking that provide alternatives to relying on a binary logic process for such discussion and decision-making.

But before exploring third way thinking, let's examine some background to the binary process.

## The Law of Non Contradiction

Plato postulated 'three laws of thought' which are fundamental factors for arguments for reasoning: (1) The Law of Identity: Two 'entities' represented as *x* and *y* are the same if they both have 'the same properties'; (2) The Law of Non Contradiction: 'Either *x* or not *x* is true' without any other option; and (3) The Law of the Excluded Middle: 'An entity *x* has or does not have a property P. Conversely, a property P is either possessed by an entity *x* or it is not possessed by *x*.'[4]

The Law of Non Contradiction means that things that are opposite of each other cannot both be true at the same time. Therefore, some form of distinction needs to be made between the two. For example, for a question such as: What is the capital of Thailand—Bangkok or Chiang Mai—the answer cannot be both. It cannot be contradictory. It is one or the other (Bangkok, not Chiang Mai).

While there are non-contradictory approaches used in Western logic, a case can be made that some in the East approach logic in a more circular or non-binary way. Some researchers, for example, suggest that East Asians do not necessarily hold a commitment to 'avoiding the appearance of contradictions'.[5] Stated another way, some cultures may treat contradictions differently than the Western method of employing Plato's laws.[6]

## Binary contrasts and choices

There is a correlation between the Law of Non Contradiction and binary logic. The word binary means, 'consisting of or involving two'.[7] In computer programming, binary means using only the digits 0 (off) and 1 (on). Binary can apply to decision-making when it involves deciding between two alternatives. For example, a binary choice can mean choosing the colour blue instead of red. Binary choice is used to evaluate reasoning skills, such that questions can be based on true/false; yes/no; correct/incorrect.

There are many binary contrasts in the Bible, several of which are listed in the following table. They are not presented as choices per se, but each contrasts the other:

| | |
|---|---|
| Heaven | Hell |
| Light | Dark(ness) |
| Faith | Unbelief |
| Blessing | Curses |
| Life | Death |
| Truth | Lies |

**Examples of Binary Contrasts in the Bible**

## Biblical examples of binary choices

Jesus asked his disciples, 'Who do people say that the Son of Man is?' (Matthew 16:13-16 NET). The disciples responded with a number of possibilities: John the Baptist, Elijah, Jeremiah or one of the prophets. Then Jesus asked, 'But who do you say that I am?' Simon Peter answered, 'You are the Christ, the Son of the living God.' In that answer, Simon Peter made a binary choice—he chose Christ over the options given.

In James 4:6, God makes a binary choice. He chooses to give his grace to the humble instead of favoring the proud (he opposes them).

There is also a binary choice that God gives to all people: by choosing life, blessings, light, salvation and Jesus we have gone through a binary selection and made a particular choice. The alternative choice is to embrace sin, which according to God results in death, eternal separation, darkness and curses.

## Further examples of binary choices

There are many different kinds of binary choices we make or create when we approach the Bible, the church, society and even in specific aspects of mission e.g. Bible translation. Here are some examples:

**Binary choices we create from the Bible:**

*Which is more important?*

| Old Testament | New Testament |
|---|---|

*Who was Jesus happiest with?*

| Mary (worship) | Martha (task) |
|---|---|

**Binary choices we create in the church:**

*Which is more important?*

| Elders | Deacons |
|---|---|
| Reformed | Charismatic |
| Proclamation of the gospel | Demonstration of the gospel |

**Binary choices in society:**

*Which is better?*

| Western | Majority world |
|---|---|
| Urban | Rural |
| Male | Female |

**Binary choices in Bible translation movements:**

*Which is more important?*

| Bible translation | Language development |
|---|---|
| Theory | Practice |
| Task | Impact |
| Starts | Finishes |
| Print | Oral |

**Examples of Binary Choices**

## A definition of mission: binary or non-binary?

No, it's not a trick question. But it can act as a reminder of how stealthily this notion of either/or instead of both/and can find a home in the mind-set of church and organizational leadership. Fortunately, the field of missiology can provide a wealth of understanding to address this issue. Missiology looks at the world from the perspective of commitment to the Christian faith. Its purpose is not the maintenance of the missionary initiative. Instead, it scrutinises the missionary enterprise's aims, attitudes, message and methods.

With that in mind, further work on establishing a non-binary understanding of mission is necessary, in order to diffuse the long-standing tension between an emphasis on evangelism or social responsibility.

For example, Van Engen offers an interim explanation, in which he attempts to accommodate various perspectives:

> Mission is the people of God intentionally crossing barriers from church to non-church, faith to non-faith, to proclaim by word and deed the coming of the kingdom of God in Jesus Christ; this task is achieved by means of the church's participation in God's mission of reconciling people to God, to themselves, to each other, and to the world, and gathering them into the church through repentance and faith in Jesus Christ by the work of the Holy Spirit with a view to the transformation of the world as a sign of the kingdom in Jesus Christ.[8]

By using the lens of missiology, leadership can learn and discern what can be most helpful in considering missional practice. Complexities associated with local, regional and global contexts mean that trends and themes affecting practice may not fit neatly into binary choices.

# Third Way Thinking

The concepts of a third place, culture, table or space are not new. However, what may be missing is the integration and application of these concepts to better understand new formats of working together in God's mission.

## Third places

Sociologists and city planners often employ the concept of a third place. This is a social surrounding separate from where one lives (first place) and where one works (second place). Examples of third places are cafes, clubs or parks. Ray Oldenburg argues that third places are important for society, and establish feelings of a sense of place. A third place offers sanctuary other than what is found in the workplace or home, where people can frequently visit and connect with friends, neighbours, colleagues and strangers.[9]

The qualities that make up a third place include: they are neutral places where people can easily come and go; they are inclusive and do not require formal membership; they are low in profile; they are open outside normal office hours; they have a 'playful mood'; they provide 'psychological comfort and support'; and they give space for conversations.[10]

Third places function as a sort of entry port for newcomers who meet those who have come before them. The idea is that in these third places, people no longer feel alone. This social mixing is needed because the first and second places make their own claims on their participants. Oldenburg summarizes the third place as 'neutral ground' that is intended to provide a level of 'social equality'.[11]

The advancement of online technology—demonstrated by increasing movement towards the Internet—means virtual third places are also important, and new ones are continually being developed. For example, multiplayer online games may be providing social connections that are functionally very similar to physical third places.[12] Proponents of this third space argue that our increasingly polarized world needs a place that brings people together across differing ideologies and political preferences.

## Third culture and TCKs

A third culture is the notion of a 'hybrid culture' because the person ably builds relationships with 'all of the cultures' without necessarily having

# Neither One Way Nor the Other

*by Bryan Harmelink*

In post-colonial studies, the concept of third space is an integral part of the writings of Homi Bhabha. He observes that, '... passage through a Third Space' results in a hybrid, which is 'neither the one thing nor the other'.*

As I reflect on this concept of third space, I find it's important to recognize that it doesn't negate the reality of either/or choices or yes/no questions that are part of everyday life. Sometimes, however, it may appear that all we have is an either/or choice. But appearances can be deceiving. For example, we often don't recognize how complex a simple disagreement can be. There may not be *just* two sides—there may be another way to resolve an issue. This is where the concept of third space may be helpful. Sometimes the best way forward, to paraphrase Bhabha's words, is *neither one way nor the other*, but rather a negotiated third way.

As an example of a third way, let's

ownership of any of them.[13] There can be aspects from each culture that are 'assimilated' into the person's experience, but the real 'sense of belonging' takes place in the person's relationships with others who share 'similar backgrounds'.[14] This results in a sense of 'rootlessness and rootedness in several cultures'.[15]

Third Culture Kid (TCK) is a term given to those who typically belong to neither their home culture (first culture or passport country) nor their host culture (second culture), but an in-between culture. Usually it means the person has spent a substantial part of 'his or her developmental years outside the parents' culture'.[16]

The origin of the term 'Third Culture Kid' is attributed to Ruth Hill Useem and John Useem, social scientists who, in the 1950s, studied Americans (first culture) living in India (second culture) as diplomats, missionaries, aid workers, educators and so forth. They also encountered expatriates of other nationalities who had their own subcultures characterized by interlocking 'peculiarities, slightly different origins, distinctive styles and stratification systems'. In other words, these expatriate communities had created their own way of living—their own 'culture between cultures' (third culture) that was different from their host Indian context, even though they shared the same environment. Ruth Useem called the children raised in this context 'Third Culture Kids'.[17]

TCKs share these two primary realities that shape who they are: they are raised in diverse 'cultural worlds' as they go back and forth between their 'passport and host cultures'; and mobility is their norm, because they either are moving or those around them are moving.[18] Living within the concept of their third culture gives them a means for identity, and empowers them to function in a meaningful way.

## Third tables

As I highlighted in the opening text of Chapter 6, the WGA has been experimenting with the concept of third tables. This involves creating a space that is neither the first table of the Western world, nor the second table of the global South and East, but instead, it is a

consider a critical point in the history of the Church and its mission. There were two deeply entrenched sides in the disagreement that led to the gathering that has been referred to as the Jerusalem Council in Acts 15 (NLT). One side stated clearly that 'The Gentile converts must be circumcised and required to follow the law of Moses' (15:5), and the other side declared that God 'accepts Gentiles by giving them the Holy Spirit' (15:8). Both sides had strong cases for their position. The Pharisees' representatives from Judea based their position on the Law of Moses (15:1), but Paul and Barnabas argued their position from 'the miraculous signs and wonders God had done through them among the Gentiles' (15:12). In defence of Paul and Barnabas, James referred to Peter's experience and quoted the prophets to argue that the Scriptures predicted exactly what Paul and Barnabas were claiming. For the Jews on both sides of this dispute, the Law of Moses was not something to be taken lightly, but the signs and wonders God was doing among the Gentiles were impossible to ignore! How could an impasse of this magnitude be resolved?

This is where the letter written by

the apostles and elders in Jerusalem comes in. Here's an excerpt of what they wrote to the Gentile believers in Antioch, Syria, and Cilicia:

> For it seemed good to the Holy Spirit and to us to lay no greater burden on you than these few requirements: You must abstain from eating food offered to idols, from consuming blood or the meat of strangled animals, and from sexual immorality. (15:28-29).

What happened to the insistence on circumcision and following the Law of Moses? While these three requirements are consistent with or found within the law (for example, Leviticus 17:10-14 on the matter of consuming blood or the meat of strangled animals), they are certainly not equivalent to being circumcised and obeying the Law. We could also ask: what happened to Paul and Barnabas' position that God accepts Gentiles by giving them the Holy Spirit? If this is the case, why should Gentile believers be given any requirements from the Law?

At this point, I recall Bhabha's description of the third space as 'neither the one thing nor the other' and consider how this describes what the letter from the apostles and elders in Acts 15 does. There was both respect for the Law and recognition of the gift of the Spirit, but neither side simply won. What emerged was a negotiated third way, a way forward that was *neither* the Pharisees' way *nor* that of Paul and Barnabas.

But—you might protest—that's different! The Holy Spirit guided them to that 'inspired' solution. True, we're not the apostles and elders of Paul's day, but the same Spirit is guiding the Church today. When we're faced with complex issues, it may appear there are only two sides, but may the Spirit give us discernment and guide us to look beyond the usual binary choices and find a third way forward.

*Homi Bhabha, *The Location of Culture* (New York: Routledge, 1994), 49.

neutral and shared space between the two which serves as a safe place to discuss and develop values that enable the global missional community to work more closely together as trusted friends.

The initial WGA-sponsored third table event, held in 2015, was called: *Leaders Journeying Together—Third Table Forum*. Todd Poulter, a facilitator for the event and WGA's consultant for leadership development, states that the original idea of the third table came from Peter

Tarantal of OM International. Twenty-seven participants from 16 nations attended, roughly split between those from the West and those from the global South and East.

Without fully describing the multi-day process, the purpose of the activity for creating a third table was to help the participants recognize and appreciate the gifts each had, despite different backgrounds, in areas such as leadership, decision-making, relationships, time orientation, use of money, use of power and authority, etc., and to bring them to the third table (the one to which everyone could contribute).

One example of the gift exchange was when the second table offered the first table the gift of 'Community—friendly and approachable', explaining it as: 'We value collective input or consultation, and community welfare is valued more than exclusive right(s)'. The African maxim of 'I am because we are' was also included. The first table readily received this gift, to the surprise and delight of the second table. By accepting the gift, the first table acknowledged that it needed help to live and be community within the global context.

The first table then offered the second table the gift of 'Dealing with conflict with love and respect in a timely manner (i.e. not avoiding or ignoring it, and leaving room for multiple ways of dealing with it)'. The second table graciously accepted the gift.

As the gift exchange came to a close, some at the event stated that this was the first time in memory that there had been a leap forward in cross-cultural learning and understanding, despite this being a relatively simple but unique process. It was the first time that most had participated in such a dialogue about what are often sensitive or overlooked inter-cultural values.

In summary, the third table gift exchange process provided a safe place to discuss and develop values that enable global missional communities to work more closely together. New space and community experiences were created that blended together Western and global South and East values and perspectives. The third table process gave all of the participants a way of practicing a genuine interest in hearing from and valuing each other, as well as sharing the gifts each had to offer.

Rather than being divided by differences, the process gave participants a means of complementing and appreciating each other.

## Third spaces

There are many examples of how sociologists and theologians have used the concept of third spaces as a metaphor for analyzing complexities facing a globalized world.

*Third space mindset:* Adam Fraser notes how the stress of modern living is requiring a readjustment to work-life balance. So much so that the objective is how to manage the 'transition between' the spaces/roles people must fulfil.[19] For example, the 'First Space is the role/environment/task we are in right now. The Second Space is the role/environment/task we are about to move into. The Third Space is the transitional gap in between the First and Second spaces'.[20] The third space is where greater balance and happiness may be found. In other words, the third space is not so much a physical place but a mental process—a mindset to get in the right frame of mind as one makes the transition between the two spaces.

*Third space social construct:* Homi Bhabha offers another type of third space. The first space is occupied by modern society and its resulting values, such as the Enlightenment contribution of unrelenting progress and individualism. Migrants who come from traditional and often closed or fundamentalist religions and societies occupy the second space. Society struggles to integrate the two into one homogenous unit, because both sides must give up something significant. What is needed is the middle or third space that respects the two, and through the political process, negotiates what this new or hybrid space should look like and how it should function. An example of this playing out in real time can be seen in various nations, especially in Europe, grappling with large influxes of refugees from war-torn regions in the Middle East.[21]

*Third space friendship:* As referenced in chapter 4, Price states a third space is needed between the West's new colonialism with its domination of resources and its cultural hegemony (or power), and those in the global South and East who live without the power and influence of financial resources.[22] A third space helps to frame a missiological understanding of friendship, which deepens the value of partnering in mission. True cross-cultural friendship requires a long-term commitment between individuals and places and includes the need to understand, respect, learn from, and live amongst another culture or religion.

*Third space church:* Christopher Baker states that third spaces enable 'the emergence of hybrid forms' through a process of 'interrogation'. In other words, we are searching for the right questions to ask each other and this in turn creates some third spaces, which are places 'for new possibilities' that 'unstick' our minds.[23] This process is designed to discover 'new patterns of Christian praxis and theology'.[24] It helps to negotiate a third space between 'post-colonial' tendencies of the Western church as it negotiates its purpose in the midst of 'postmodern urban space and civil society'.[25] Rather than relying on past 'top-down methodologies' inherent in the Christendom church, there is currently the need to 'engage with a multiplicity of influences that now compete with each other on equal terms'.[26] What third space brings into the equation is 'an acceptance of diversity... and a willingness to embrace the concept of hybridity'.[27] This helps the church overcome its fear of 'the Other', or the outsider, who is an outcome of polarization from disparate socio-economic factors associated with global capitalism.[28] What may emerge is a third space church with the promise of 'a commitment to partnership and reconciliation'.[29] This third space is needed between our postmodern secular culture and our culture's perceptions of the church as an exclusive club removed from the relevance of modern society.

## Third spaces and systems theory

Coertze raises a relevant point on thinking about third spaces from the perspective of systems theory:

> D. S. Becvar and R. J. Becvar provide a basic explanation for the meaning of systems theory. 'In the world of systems theory... the notion of linear causality is not meaningful. Instead we find an emphasis on reciprocity... and shared responsibility.' So in the context of a relationship in which each person influences the other

equally, as we look at this relationship from the outside, and seek to understand issues or events within the relationship, we would not ask *why something happened*, but rather *what is going on* in this relationship.[30]

Another way in which we can differentiate between a linear causality way of functioning and functioning in a systems theory context is in our method of counting within a family, as an example. In linear causality, a single person, or 'space', if you will, is counted as one. That person marries, and now they are two. They have a child, and now they are three.

In systems theory, a single person is one. However, that person marries, and now they are three. They have a child and now they are nine. How does this way of counting actually work in systems theory? When the man and woman marry, they add a 'third space', as they develop an identity together. It is in this third space that they learn to function as a married couple. Likewise, when a child is born, the child/father relationship creates another third space and the child/mother relationship creates yet another third space, which leads to a total of nine spaces within this family unit.[31]

**Third Spaces in a Family**

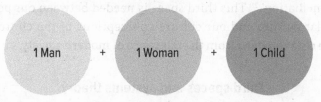

= **3** People (Spaces) in Linear Causality

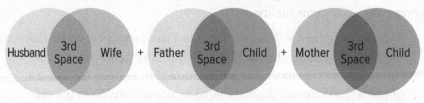

= **9** Spaces in Systems Theory

## Christ as the perfect third space

Is Jesus Christ the ultimate example of third space? Paul writes in Romans 5:8 (NET), 'God demonstrates his own love for us, in that while we were still sinners, Christ died for us.' When Christ became the bridge between God and humanity, as God's son sent to die and reconcile and reunite us to God, did he become—and does he continue to be—the perfect third space?

The writer of Hebrews refers to Jesus Christ as 'the mediator of a new covenant, so that those who are called may receive the eternal inheritance he has promised, since he died to set them free from the violations committed under the first covenant' (Hebrews 9:15 NET). The Apostle Paul refers in this way to Jesus' mediator role: 'For there is one God and one intermediary between God and humanity, Christ Jesus, himself human' (1 Timothy 2:5 NET). This speaks to the go-between role that Jesus plays. In the third space metaphor, Jesus is the mediator between God (the first space) and humanity (the second space). Jesus occupies this third space.

We see in Jesus' relationship with the Samaritans a different approach than that of the prevailing culture. Again, using the third space metaphor, Jesus acts in the third space in his encounter with a Samaritan woman (John 4). Jesus' conversation with her demonstrated how the gospel overcomes all barriers. Jesus becomes the example of entering into a new space when he overlooked four Jewish traditions: (1) speaking to a woman (men were not to even look at a married woman in public let alone talk to them); (2) relating to a promiscuous person (rabbis and holy men fled from such people); (3) being with a Samaritan (Jews were forbidden to speak with Samaritans); and (4) accepting a drink from an 'unclean' person (due to her menstruation, anything a woman touched was considered to be unclean, and handing Jesus a container of water would make Jesus unclean by accepting it).

Jesus' acceptance of the woman from Samaria resulted in her pursuing her spiritual thirst. Jesus' treatment of her was typical of how he viewed all people—he elevated them to authentic personhood, and showed that they were worthy of respect and God's love. She is the only person in the Gospels who receives the honour of hearing the Messiah identify himself in the first person, 'I who speak to you am he' (John 4:26 RSV). This encounter between Jesus and the woman of Samaria gives us a good example of someone (Jesus) operating in a third space.

## The rule of thirds

In my background as a photographer, I learned about the rule of thirds, which applies to the process of composing photographs. Picture an image divided into nine equal parts using two vertical lines and two horizontal lines. Positioning a subject at intersection points of those lines provides more interest than simply centering the subject. When viewing photographs, most people's eyes go to one of the intersection points rather than to the centre of the image. Thus, using the rule of thirds works with this natural way of viewing, rather than against it.

Making the comparison to third spaces, those intersection points within a well-composed photograph form a pleasing space within a space—a third space, if you will, where the photographer and the subject, while separate, find a 'meeting space' within the photographic frame. This shared third space allows for enhanced understanding about both the photographer and the subject, and one can learn and appreciate more about each because of this placement.

After 15 years in global ministry, I find myself seeking natural intersection points that allow for enhanced understanding and new appreciation for others as we serve in God's mission together.

The challenge for global missional leadership is to find the third spaces, to create the third table, and discern unexpected discoveries and solutions that we could not see clearly before.

# Questions for Consideration and Discussion

1. In your small group, discuss some examples of binary choices you make in relation to your ministry—or binary choices made by leadership within the context of your church or mission agency.

2. Discuss some ideas of third spaces that could be helpful in your ministry as you serve in partnership with others, or within the framework of your church or organization.

3. Jesus is described in the chapter as the ultimate example of third space. Within the context of your small group or team, describe what that means to you.

# Forming a Global Missional Mindset

In December 2007, the newly appointed leadership team for Wycliffe International (before it became WGA) met for the first time in Singapore. We came with our spouses for three days and had these goals: get to know each other better so we can support each other as a team, make plans and pray together in preparation to begin as the new leadership team.

Most of us did not know each other. Most of the roles were brand new. So, we answered this question: What should characterize our team? We compiled a long list of values that can be summarized in two groups: (1) *How we work together*: We respect each other with good interpersonal relationships and open communication, celebration and trust. We are known by our fellowship and partnership, are outward looking and respect diversity. We are flexible, cope with change and are responsive to the opportunities God gives us. We eliminate 'silos' that take shape within our structure. We have alignment with each other in what we say internally and externally because we integrate our thinking within the whole team. We are always learning from one another and from our partners. (2) *The kind of leadership we provide*: We reveal godliness through praying together and are sensitive to the Holy Spirit. We demonstrate Christ's love in all we do and say. We are servant leaders and develop credibility with others, internally and externally. We are visionary and creative. We are good and effective partners with a wider concern than just our own people, strategies and programs. We are people of both action and reflection.

From the outset, there are some commendable characteristics that this new team sought to accomplish. Did we succeed? Have we been able to maintain our values of how we work together and the kind of leadership we provide?

The best way I can answer that is to recount something I did in June 2016. The leadership team was together for its biannual face-to-face meeting. At the very end of our five days together, I shared from my heart about how I was doing at the time. I told of many different and often-interrelating factors that had begun to engulf me in my leadership role. Most were really good things—fruitfulness of the past eight years. However, I had become unbalanced. My travel schedule was overwhelming and meant I was too often away from home. There were more demands upon my time for writing and speaking than I could fit in. I had just graduated with my PhD and the exhilaration of finishing left me feeling empty, which was something I had not anticipated, and added to my sense of unease at the time.

At the end of my sharing, the leadership team opened up with words of encouragement, concern, appreciation, and suggestions on what I—and we—could do differently. With their help and support, I immediately cancelled some upcoming engagements. At the very end we stood in a circle and prayed, and then I asked those present for a group hug. One person who has been on the team from the outset observed, 'You've never asked for a group hug before!' He was grateful I had come to this point in my journey. The hug was symbolic to me of the leadership community we're becoming. What we set out to create in 2007 continues to mature. This was obvious through my taking the risk to be more vulnerable and share at a deeper personal level with this team I work with and lead. I experienced the love and support of a group of leaders who demonstrated their understanding of leading with a global missional heart and mindset.

## Residue, Leadership Heritage, Spirituality and Power

Now those are four unlikely traveling companions to begin our journey with in this final chapter, which is devoted to shining light on an emerging paradigm shift towards global missional leadership. But all have a role in helping us proceed on our journey, and can contribute to our learning about the changing dynamics of leadership in global settings.

Let's begin with what remains.

## Residue

It's not so much the reality of sometimes-messy aspects of global ministry that gets my attention. Rather, it's the realization that while on a journey through this reality, it is the *residue* of such messiness that can have unanticipated value and importance, and shouldn't be overlooked.

Among other nuances of meaning, residue represents something remaining—something leftover as a result of a particular process. And it need not carry a negative connotation.

For example, in a 20th century model of institutional organizational leadership, an emphasis on making strategic plans tidy and properly categorized would be apparent. In contrast, 21st century global realities virtually assure leadership that untidy remains resulting from a planning process will be the new norm. But those remains can be the key to finding a way forward. Let me illustrate.

Drawing again from my photography background, a now long-outdated method of visual presentation was the slideshow, with images projected on a screen via one or more slide projectors, often accompanied by a soundtrack. Creating the slideshow began at a light table. One would gather together the 35mm slides on this surface, arranging them for projection, to tell a basic visual story. More than once when arranging the images I was convinced I had the order correct on the light table, but when projecting them, something just wasn't right. So I'd go back to the light table and look at the leftover slides. Inevitably, inserting one or more of these into the slideshow created just the right balance. Alone on the light table, these remnant images seemed without much value, according to my original thought process. But once integrated into the fuller presentation, they became the key to the slideshow—not because they were the best photos I had taken, but because of their placement within a larger setting, and how they worked in concert alongside the others.

Let us now look at some leadership heritage that has shaped church and organizational thinking, and how globalization impacts traditional leadership models.

## Studies and models of leadership

There are volumes of studies on leadership behaviours, principles and traits, whether from a business, not-for-profit, Christian mission or church perspective, and sometimes a combination of some or all of these. Within the framework of leading in the context of the *missio Dei*, several leadership types are pertinent to mission in a global setting. These include: (1) the transformational leader who encourages creative ideas and intellectual stimulation that broadens and challenges followers to move beyond their self-interests to what is best for the whole group;[1] (2) the servant leader who leads by example and whose attitude of serving others develops trust;[2] (3) the shepherd leader who compassionately uses diverse skills and techniques according to the needs of the context;[3] and (4) the missional leader who understands that it is through God's grace that one participates in leading in God's mission.[4] All of these types may also be blended together to give dynamic global missional leadership.

However, most common leadership practices in global mission appear to be based upon Western biases for their orientation of leadership. Leadership and organizational theories formulated in the West do not always have application to other cultures.[5] For example, Robert Banks and Bernice Ledbetter give an extensive overview of contemporary approaches of Christian leadership using sources only from Western authors and publishers.[6] Even with the interconnected influences of globalization, it is possible for Western scholarship in the domain of leadership to be far removed from global South and East contexts that create new challenges not necessarily anticipated by Western models. As Christianity makes its home in the soil of the non-Western world, it does not mean that Western forms of Christianity have lost their relevancy; rather, the Christian faith is truly a universal one. But it seems apparent that these Western-based leadership methods are inadequate to serve the purposes of church and missional approaches in changing contexts that are interconnected, multi-religious, multi-cultural and inter-cultural.

## Globalization's effect on domestic leadership models

Allen Morrison argues that globalization places immense pressure on organizations and companies to quickly develop international approaches. However, this requires leaders who have not developed only within domestic contexts. Instead, global leaders need a broader and cross-cultural leadership model to understand specific cultural contexts.[7] According to Morrison, this is inadequate as well because leadership models from one country do not usually work in another part of the world.[8] There are too many variables, such as 'relationships, short-term profits, hierarchies, ethics and risk'.[9]

While globalization has become the world's reality, the concept of global leadership has not received the same attention that domestic leadership has. When considering domestic leadership models, most literature focuses on the US and other Western contexts. For example, Ernest Gundling et al. summarize Kotter's definition of leadership (see *John P. Kotter on What Leaders Really Do*, 1999), as generally domestic in concept. It 'involves coping with change by setting direction, aligning people, and motivating and inspiring—often through leveraging informal networks within the organization'.[10] But Kotter's definition of leadership seems inadequate when applied to a globalized context. For example, Gundling et al. note that Kotter does not address issues like interpreting markets in different local contexts across the globe, creating vision in those same contexts, or communicating with people with diverse nationalities who have different communication styles.[11]

Globalization complicates leadership because of the diversity of challenges in a globalized world, the interdependence of multiple human and technological systems and infrastructures across the globe, and ambiguity that arises from a diversity of factors, whether they are cross-cultural or result from how information is interpreted.[12] Morrison believes that global leaders must learn how to overcome familiar national distinctions and integrate 'best practices' from around the world into their practices.[13]

It follows that the depth and complexity of global issues facing church and mission leadership today cannot be ignored. And it is problematic to succinctly express formulas for successful missional leadership in global contexts. Further, instead of modifying existing models of leadership, there is critical need to ask what the new paradigm for global missional leadership is looking like thus far. It is my view that we are now in the beginning of such a paradigm shift.

As part of an examination of this developing new leadership paradigm, we should consider a key foundational basis for the formation of a global missional mindset: spirituality.

## Spirituality

Understanding spirituality means we must reflect upon 'the practices and beliefs of the religion with which it is connected'.[14] Therefore, Christian missional leadership looks to Christ as the ultimate missional leadership example and inspiration. It follows that the spiritual maturity and transformation of the leader and follower is of paramount importance. Thus, the definition of Christian spirituality given by Larry Richards is fitting: 'living a human life... in union with God'.[15] This life has been practiced throughout the ages as a 'companionship with Jesus' as one draws life from a 'conversational relationship with God'.[16]

Mature spirituality requires 'self-awareness and openness to God'.[17] It is not concerned simply with spiritual disciplines and habits. Rather, 'spirituality is informed by the *missio Dei* and the theological reflection of the church'.[18]

Additionally, Scott Sunquist identifies seven practices and beliefs that are fundamental for spiritual formation in Christian mission: (1) silence: the 'secret' of the spiritual life is to learn to wait upon the Holy Spirit, who provides his gifts to enable participation in his mission; (2) learning and memorizing Scripture; (3) community: spirituality is 'nurtured in submission to others'; (4) repentance 'opens the doorway to spiritual power [through] honest weakness'; (5) action: a 'gentle dance of the personal and communal, of silence and action, and of study and reflection'; (6) attentiveness: learning to pay attention to the needs around oneself; and (7) love, because without it a missional life is like 'a resounding gong or a clanging cymbal' (1 Corinthians 13:1).[19]

**Sunquist's Foundations for Spiritual Formation in Christian Mission**

## Spirituality in mission is context-sensitive

Missional spirituality takes place in, and is deeply influenced within, a cultural context. As God works around the world, we hear stories and descriptions of what spirituality looks like in God's people. These stories provide tangible learning experiences about the rich diversity of spirituality, spiritual practices and traditions and remind us of the diversity in God's mission.

Take, for example, missionary preparation in the era of the 1910 Edinburgh World Missionary Conference. At that time, preparation focused on the 'quality of spirituality' that became evident in missionary training. The process was meant to cultivate 'a deeply rooted spiritual life... where God rather than self was the actual centre'.[20]

Throughout mission history, renewal and expansion of the Christian faith is accompanied by new spiritual dynamics and revitalized forms of spirituality. The intensive missionary efforts over the past 100 years have demonstrated this as 'the strongholds of Christian spirituality' shifting from the West to the global South and East.[21]

Monks in the monastic movement understood there was no such thing as a 'quick-fix mentality' in spirituality in mission, because mission spans from one generation to the next.[22] The church in God's mission might see temporary progress, but without 'a spirituality of the long haul', it might not be sustained.[23] Mature missional spirituality 'is the source of energy for mission' brought through the transformative Holy Spirit.[24]

Spirituality thus becomes an important component seen in the unfolding paradigm shift towards global missional leadership.

But I would be remiss in describing factors relating to leadership—no matter from what era or paradigm—without addressing the topics of power and authority. The changing nature of power and authority affects all forms of global leadership, in particular what leaders do. The effects are great, and it is important to establish the major concerns.

## Shifts in power and authority

Naim Moises defines power as what is exercised over others that causes them to act in ways they would not otherwise have acted.[25] Hans Morgenthau describes power as 'anything that establishes and maintains the control' of one person over another.[26] Simon Reich and Richard Lebow add that power operates in a context, so leaders need 'physical or moral resources' in order to influence others.[27] Ronald Heifetz et al. note that power and authority are 'critical tools' for leadership, but should not define it.[28]

Barbara Kellerman claims that the only leaders today who are free from the limits of power are the 'tyrannical' ones who willingly and ably use power to intimidate. For the remainder, there are numerous limits on their ability to exert power, authority and influence.[29] It follows that those in power are noticing that their power is now more 'feeble, transient and constrained'.[30]

There are additional limitations on how power is used today, such as the capacity to retain privacy against the prying eyes of a public that wants to know everything, or the pressure to perform to a certain standard. When outcomes do not measure up to expectations, termination may be quickly arranged. Communication technologies allow immediate access to all kinds of information, in particular, social media platforms for self-expression. This means that practically everyone everywhere is able to critique a leader's performance, and in effect belittle the leader through 'disclosures of personal information'.[31] Leaders can now be quickly exposed as dishonest, foolish, incompetent, self-indulgent, corrupt, and so forth.[32] The Millennial generation (born in the 1980s-1990s) in particular is more sceptical of institutions and individuals and very comfortable in the digitalized global world. They therefore are ready and willing to challenge authority, whether directly, but certainly indirectly, through social media.[33]

## Dysfunctional organizations

Leaders respond to challenges in different ways. One way is when the leader acts as the pragmatic 'hero' who copies the prevailing leadership practices and uses them to exert 'power through control'. This leader's focus is upon achieving concrete results. Another type of leader acts as the artistic 'sceptic' who deconstructs through 'creativity and novelty'. The hero or sceptical leaders deeply affect the institutions they lead through the loss of 'prophetic voice' that is needed in wider cultural and interconnected contexts. The end result may be fatigue, discouragement and paralysis of the leader, as well as for the institutions they lead.[34]

Organizations tend to adopt the characteristics of their key leaders. In 'addictive' organizations, the leader behaves like an 'active addict' with behaviours that may be depressive, paranoid and compulsive. Consequently, the leader has great influence by drawing attention to himself or herself, and this soon becomes a drain on others.[35]

Further, leaders are easily able to 'paint their own dysfunction' over the organizations they lead. In such cases, leadership is about 'appeasing fears and insecurities [to] gain a sense of personal meaning'. This can result in the promotion of 'workaholism' and is of particular danger for the church and Christian organizations, perhaps due to the concept of the industrious Protestant work ethic.[36] This type of leadership is also associated with the capitalistic economic system that undergirds it.[37]

## A new social contract

A long-established 'social contract' has existed between leaders and followers in which the leader (regardless of what type) is normally expected to 'control the action' and the follower is expected to 'go along' with it.[38] However, due to shifting understandings of power and authority, the conventions on which the contract is based are being tested.

Moises notes that power is deteriorating because it is 'easier to get, harder to use and easier to lose'.[39] Those with power are more constrained in the ways they can use it. The technological acumen of interconnected people is the fuel for this shift. These powers of technology enable new players to 'feel entitled and act emboldened' and speak their mind, regardless of the consequences.[40] As influence spreads, newer and smaller players are challenging the traditional players of power. Moises calls these the 'micropowers' that are decentralized with nimble players that find ways to 'undermine, fence in, or thwart the megaplayers'.[41] One only needs to scan news headlines to see how underground computer hacking groups, or 'hacktivists', can create disruption across any border.

This increasing uncertainty causes leaders to act with a short-term focus, with fewer reasons to develop longer-term strategies.[42] The IT 'evangelists' who overstate that technology will solve all problems also tend to exaggerate their claims and end up being part of the dilemma.[43]

## Leadership development considerations

Developing 'contextual intelligence' is the new key, according to Kellerman. It is now 'knowledge about and understanding the context' that is of crucial importance for leadership.[44]

Kellerman finds that the leadership development industry is ill equipped to deal with the new contexts because it has been 'self-satisfied, self-perpetuating, and poorly policed'.[45] She further states that 'leadership as an area of intellectual inquiry' is undeveloped because of minimal innovative thought given to what 'leader learning' needs to encompass. There also has been little thought given to instruction about 'following wisely' as being as important as leading well.[46]

In the haste for efficiency in leadership development, Kellerman suggests that leader learning has been 'condensed and contracted' to meet the call for instant gratification, which is the feature of this century.[47] The cultural storms affecting leadership reduce confidence in power and influence.

Into this milieu, Sayers offers an alternative: the need for creative leader-influencers 'who have met [God] in the storm' and are ready to be 'partners with God' in the transformation of God's creation.[48] This is a very different perspective for leadership development than many existing models.

## Forming a Global Missional Mindset

Forming a mindset can sound somewhat clinical. But as we've seen in the preceding chapters, understanding what it means to be part of a global community, to work and pray, live and serve with one another in God's mission, is anything but clinical.

And most importantly, the process is ongoing, refined and informed via openness to the Holy Spirit.

As I reflect on this topic, my experience and study have shown that a synthesis of characteristics from both missional and global leadership frameworks, attributes stemming from complexity leadership theory, along with key leadership values, are leading factors in the formation of a global missional mindset.

### Missional leadership characteristics

As discussed in Chapter 1, missional leaders help the church take her place in God's story[49] and participate in the triune God's mission of transformation.[50] These leaders empower people to develop an imagination of what God is doing. Such leadership must be courageous, equipped with

**Leading Factors in the Formation of a Global Missional Mindset**

biblical and theological mindsets, coupled with the ability to understand the changing cultural context around them.[51]

This is foundational in the formation of a global missional mindset precisely because of the characteristics of missional leadership:

- discerning with the Holy Spirit and God's community what God is doing in the world;
- dwelling in God's word and living within the narrative of Scripture;
- imagining what God wants to do in the world; and
- an inner transformation of the leader and those he or she leads.[52]

## Global leadership characteristics

Philip Harris et al. define global leadership as

being capable of operating effectively in a global environment while being respectful of cultural diversity. This is an individual who can manage accelerating change and differences. The global leader is open and flexible in approaching others, can cope with situations and people disparate from his or her own background, and is willing to re-examine and alter personal attitudes and perceptions.[53]

Gundling et al. developed five behaviours crucial for global leaders in complex situations across multiple geographic and cultural contexts, which I summarize as follows:

- Identifying differences that really matter (i.e. global leaders must be able to sift through a myriad of situations and find the issues that are essential for success);
- Creating strong personal relationships between themselves and those they work with in other cultures;
- Finding ways to enlarge ownership of solutions across numerous boundaries, which includes developing emerging leaders from various contexts;
- Maintaining balance by knowing when to adapt to local situations and when to exercise one's expertise, authority or position; and
- Finding solutions across boundaries (cultural, linguistic, organizational, etc.) or utilizing any or all five behaviours to create solutions.[54]

This brief look at characteristics of global leaders reveals how these attributes are an important component in the formation of a global missional mindset.

## Complexity leadership attributes

Complexity leadership theory distinguishes between leadership and leaders because its model of leadership is emergent, dynamic and adaptive.[55] It is not just the act of an influential individual(s) but, rather, is rooted in a multifaceted relationship that involves numerous different factors.[56] It enables the use of 'intellectual assets' through a network of 'distributed intelligence' instead of relying on the 'limited intelligence' of a few people in top-level leadership positions.[57]

The benefits of adding attributes from complexity leadership theory as a component in the formation of a global missional mindset include:

- Recognizing the advantage of a fast-responding community of leaders and teams;
- Looking for creative solutions to complex situations;
- Not maintaining the status quo; and
- Reliance upon interconnected relational teams of people responding to diverse challenges.

## Leadership values

In 2013, in an effort to gain insights based on experience working with the global leadership team for WGA, 15 team members wrote their personal leadership philosophies. A process was then followed to develop a set of leadership values through the synthesis of key themes, words and phrases of this sampling.

The values emphasize relational priorities for a leader, and thus are vital as a component in the formation of a global missional mindset. Further, the relational aspect of these values makes them suitable for any leadership environment where there is a focus on creating, building and affirming community as a leadership priority, especially in a multi-cultural and inter-cultural context.

The leadership values are:

- Relationship with Christ and reliance upon God's word: Practice personal devotion through prayer and guidance from the Bible to discern God's will in all contexts. Before a leader can 'speak God's word [he or she] must encounter the word'.[58] This is 'Biblical leadership [because] the biblical leader is a symbol who lives at the intersection of God's breaking into history'.[59]
- Christ is the ultimate leadership example: Lead as a 'first follower' of Christ—willing to lead in and from 'unconventional and unfamiliar' ways.[60]
- Align with God's missional plan: Understand God's missional heart as one faithfully uses his/her spiritual gifts in leadership.
- Commit to spiritual transformation: Live a spiritually intimate life in Christ based upon personal holiness, integrity, spiritual renewal and guidance from the Holy Spirit.
- Always learn and grow: Model servant leadership and aim for one's full potential in God's kingdom while developing wisdom and discernment through life-long learning.
- Develop other leaders: A commitment to develop other leaders and nurture them personally and by encouraging professional development.

- Value people and treat them with respect: Create a safe and trusting environment with respect and value of others who have different gifts, ethnic and church backgrounds, so that they can flourish and reach their full potential.
- Nourish a flourishing community: Value community in God's kingdom and commit to building harmonious relationships of trust.
- Face the challenges and demands of leadership: Cultivate a global perspective while leading with humility, honesty, openness and transparency in the midst of global-regional-local complexity. Schaef and Fassel note that leadership is first of all, 'a model of self-responsibility'.[61] Sayers notes that when leaders realize they cannot do anything in their own power, only then does a new type of power arise from their life[62]—'they gain spiritual authority [because] selfless leadership opens a space for God'.[63]
- Communicate with integrity: Communicate regularly and clearly one's core values through an alignment of one's words and actions.[64]

A valid observation at this point would be to wonder just how many people in this world are actually capable of possessing—and maintaining—all these characteristics, attributes and values exhibited in a global missional mindset.

But it's not a checklist. God didn't design his mission with unconnected individuals. As discussed in Chapter 3, polycentric centres of influence help guide our understanding of the need for leaders in community, which can equate to leadership-in-community, with the benefit of manifesting a *cumulative* global missional mindset.

## Global Missional Leadership—a Brief Review

This new paradigm of global missional leadership is transformational, both at a personal level and at an organizational level, because it depends on the Holy Spirit's empowerment to release an innovative spiritual gift of leadership in the church to participate in God's mission across the globe for the transformation of people in global, regional and local contexts. This leadership upholds ethical and personal integrity in the midst of a diverse range of behaviours and practices.

This leadership is not committed to maintaining the status quo, and therefore recognizes the benefits of enabling a fast-responding network of communities of leaders and teams as it searches for creative solutions to complex situations.

This leadership leads effectively within complex global environments that require the respect of cultural diversity, the ability to manage change quickly, and the discernment to interpret complex sets of information and situations. It is reliant upon interconnected relational teams of people responding to diverse challenges. It builds resilient relationships across a multitude of religious, geographic, cultural, linguistic and socio-economic boundaries.

It is my hope that this paradigm, still early along in its journey, will encourage and enable the formation of a larger pool of leaders-in-community with a global missional heart and mindset.

# Questions for Consideration and Discussion

1. Consider how power and authority in the leadership of your church, organization or team is demonstrated. Discuss within your small group how this helps and/or hinders key ministry goals.

2. Near the end of the chapter there is a listing of leadership values. Among your small group, choose several of these and discuss them in terms of your own experiences from within your organization or church or mission agency.

3. As a small group, consider the last section of this chapter. Discuss any elements of a shift towards global missional leadership that may be underway within your own contexts.

## ACKNOWLEDGEMENTS

Perhaps you have heard the African proverb, 'It takes a village to raise a child'. It is reported to come from the Igbo and Yoruba people of Nigeria. The idea is that raising a child is a communal effort. Responsibility is shared with the extended family and even wider community. Everyone participates. This proverb is similar in concept to one from the Bible—'Two people are better than one, because they can reap more benefit from their labor.... Moreover, a three-stranded cord is not quickly broken' (Ecclesiastes 4:9,12 NET).

I have had the help of a 'village' in producing this book. Here are some of the people who have helped me:

This book is the culmination of postgraduate studies under Prof C.J.P. (Nelus) Niemandt at the University of Pretoria, South Africa. I am indebted to him for his encouragement and support throughout the entire phase of my research. His closing words to me at my PhD graduation were, 'I hope you will take your research and write a book from it'.

My wife Christine has provided reassurance along the way. Her support and belief in me never wavered through the intense times when I wondered if I really could do the research and writing that was required of me, all while leading a global mission organization. Likewise, my parents, Dr Karl and Joice Franklin, gave me support and encouragement throughout this journey. During the final two-month PhD writing phase in 2015, I would send my dad, who lives in Texas, a draft of a chapter when I finished for the day. And, because of time zone differences, he would edit and comment on it while I was asleep and have it back to me by the time I woke up. I would then do the revisions and further work, and repeat the process. His academic and editorial experience meant he could quickly and incisively give me helpful input. His guidance on the thesis then made transitioning it into a book possible.

The Board of Directors and the leadership team of the Wycliffe Global Alliance have been a steady source of backing during my research, and then the writing and production of this book. They also were some of the subjects of my research. Some have written essays that accompany the chapters in this book. I am grateful to them for sharing from their wisdom, experience and insights.

The finished book has only come about because of the collaborative thought and editing attention brought by Dave and Deborah Crough. I have known them for 30 years, and we worked together on an earlier book (*Any Given Day in the Life of the Bible*). I knew when I asked them to take on this project they would do so with professionalism, diligence, faithfulness and commitment.

Finally, without the strength and source of my faith in Jesus Christ, all of the wisdom and the experiences that support or illustrate that wisdom lack meaning and relevance.

# APPENDIX

# Chapter Essay Contributors

## Chapter 1

### Stephen Coertze

Stephen was born in South Africa and resides there with his wife, Lezelle. They have two adult children.

He completed an LTh (Hons) at the Afrikaanse Baptiste Seminarium in 1989. He further completed an MA (Theology) with honours, and a PhD in missiology at the University of Pretoria.

After a period of pastoral ministry and lecturing in missiology, he joined the ministry of Bible translation. Beginning in 1997, he served as the Director for Wycliffe Bible Translators, South Africa, for over 10 years. He currently holds the role of Director for Missiology on the WGA leadership team.

## Chapter 2

### Rahab Mŭndara and Mŭndara Mŭturi

Mŭndara and Rahab were both born and raised in Kenya. They have been married for 28 years and have two adult daughters.

Mŭndara served in several leadership roles in *Bible Translation and Literacy* (a Kenyan Bible translation organization) since 1988.

He is currently serving as the Africa Area Director for WGA. He holds a BA degree in Literature and Political Science from the University of Nairobi, and postgraduate diplomas in Communications and Human Resource Management.

Rahab has both a BA degree, and a post-graduate BA degree in economics from the University of Nairobi, and an MA in Economic Planning and Public Policy from the University of Birmingham, UK. She has worked in several economic planning positions for the Kenyan government and for other development agencies. She currently works as a consultant in urban transportation.

Mŭndara and Rahab reside in Nairobi, and are active in their local church, where Mŭndara serves as an elder, and Rahab serves in premarital counseling and mentoring of newlywed couples.

# Chapter 3

### Nydia García-Schmidt

Originally from Mexico, Nydia has lived in Indonesia, the Philippines and the US. She is married to Jim Schmidt and they have three adult sons.

Nydia began theological studies at age sixteen in Mexico. She completed a BA in Christian Education from Rio Grande Bible Institute in 1991, and then earned a Master's degree in Intercultural Leadership from Crown College in 2012.

Nydia has served in several leadership capacities in WGA since 2003, and has been the Americas Area Director since 2013. She currently lives in Mexico City.

# Chapter 4

### Susan Van Wynen

Susan Van Wynen is Director for Strategy with WGA. She previously served with Wycliffe for many years in various communication and strategy leadership roles. She is a graduate of Moody Bible Institute and Biola University with a BA in Communication, and has an MA in Organizational Leadership from Azusa Pacific University. Susan and her husband, Tom, and family lived in India, Kenya and Brazil before relocating to the US.

# Chapter 5

### Minyoung Jung

Minyoung was born and raised in Korea. In the 1980's and 1990's he served a tribal people group in Papua, Indonesia as a Bible translator. Beginning in 2002 and until recently, he has contributed in various capacities, and been part of the leadership team for Wycliffe International (which later became WGA). He and his wife, Jaejin, have three adult children living on three continents.

# Chapter 6

### José de Dios

José was born in Guatemala, and has lived many years in Costa Rica and the United States. He holds a Bachelor's degree in Psychology from the University of California at Irvine. He currently lives near Dallas, Texas with Laura, his wife, and their four children. José serves as the International Coordinator of IPA (International Partnering Associates), and is a Partnering Consultant for WGA. He was involved with the work of *Generosity Path* in Latin America in 2016, engaging with givers as well as church and mission leaders around the world.

# Chapter 7

### Bryan Harmelink

After completing an MA in Linguistics from the University of Texas at Arlington, Bryan served in Chile with the Mapuche translation team (1985-1995), and participated in numerous research projects focused on Mapuche language and culture. Following the publication of the Mapuche New Testament, Bryan completed an MA in Biblical Studies and a PhD in Hermeneutics and Biblical Interpretation at Westminster Theological Seminary. Bryan has served as the Americas Area Translation Coordinator, and International Translation Coordinator for SIL International. He currently serves as Director for Collaboration with WGA.

Bryan and his wife Joan live near Philadelphia, PA. They have three adult children.

# NOTES

## Introduction

[1] Alan Roxburgh and Fred Romanuk, *The Missional Leader: Equipping Your Church to Reach a Changing World* (San Francisco: Josey-Bass, 2006), 7.

[2] Robert P. Vecchio, ed., *Understanding the Dynamics of Power and Influence in Organizations* (Notre Dame: University of Notre Dame Press, 1997), 477.

[3] John Dominic Crossan, *God and Empire: Jesus Against Rome, Then and Now* (New York: Harper, 2007), 190.

## Chapter 1: The Triune God and the *Missio Dei*

[1] Andrew Walls, "Demographics, Power and the Gospel in the 21st Century" (paper presented at the Wycliffe International Convention and the SIL International Conference, Waxhaw, 2002), 1.

[2] Lesslie Newbigin, *The Open Secret: An Introduction to the Theology of Mission*, rev. ed. (Grand Rapids: Wm. B. Eerdmans Publishing Company, 1995), 29.

[3] Timothy Tennent, *Invitation to World Missions* (Grand Rapids: Kregel, 2010), 67.

[4] Newbigin, *The Open Secret*, 65.

[5] Ibid., 29.

[6] Tennent, *Invitation to World Missions*, 67.

[7] David Bosch, *Transforming Mission: Paradigm Shifts in Theology of Mission*, 20th anniversary ed. (Maryknoll: Orbis Books, 2011), 192.

[8] Jonathan Bonk, *Missions and Money*, revised and expanded (Maryknoll: Orbis Books, 2006b), 17.

[9] Jehu Hanciles, *Beyond Christendom: Globalization, African Migration, and the Transformation of the West* (Maryknoll: Orbis Books, 2008), 85.

[10] Philip Jenkins, *The Next Christendom: The Coming of Global Christianity*, 3rd ed. (New York: Oxford University Press, 2011), 5.

[11] Tennent, *Invitation to World Missions*, 59.

[12] Michael W. Goheen, *Introducing Christian Mission Today: Scripture, History and Issues* (Downers Grove: IVP Academic, 2014), 77.

[13] Ibid., 26.

[14] Robert L. Gallagher, "Missionary Methods: The Questions That Still Dog Us," in *Missionary Methods: Research, Reflections and Realities*, eds. Craig Ott and J.D. Payne (Pasadena: William Carey Library, 2013), 4.

[15] Goheen, *Christian Mission Today*, 39.

[16] Alan Roxburgh, "Rethinking Trinitarian Missioloy," in *Global Missiology for the 21st Century: The Iguassu Dialogue*, ed. William D. Taylor (Grand Rapids: Baker Academic, 2000), 180.

[17] Tennent, *Invitation to World Missions*, 54.

[18] Ibid., 59.

[19] Roxburgh, "Rethinking Trinitarian Missioloy," 180.

[20] Bosch, *Transforming Mission: Paradigm Shifts*, 2011:402.

[21] Stephen Bevans and Roger Schroeder, *Constants in Context: A Theology for Mission Today* (Maryknoll: Orbis Books, 2004), 303.

[22] Bosch, *Transforming Mission: Paradigm Shifts*, 2011:399; Christopher Wright, *The Mission of God: Unlocking the Bible's Grand Narratives*, (Downers Grove: IVP Academic, 2006), 63.

[23] Francis Anekwe Oborji, *Concepts of Mission: The Evolution of Contemporary Missiology* (Maryknoll: Orbis, 2006), 134.

[24] Ibid., 140.

[25] Ibid.

[26] Bosch, *Transforming Mission: Paradigm Shifts*, 2011:482.

[27] Enoch Wan, "The Trinitarian Nature of the Mission of God," in *The Mission of God: Essays and Letters*, eds. Ed Stetzer and Philip Nation (Nashville: LifeWay Press, 2015), 35.

[28] Thomas Kemper, "The *Missio Dei* in Contemporary Context," *International Bulletin of Missionary Research* 38, no. 4 (2014):188.

[29] David Bosch, *Transforming Mission: Paradigm Shifts in the Theology of Mission* (Maryknoll: Orbis, 1991), 1.

[30] Kemper, "The *Missio Dei* in Contemporary Context," 188.

[31] Kirsteen Kim, *Joining in with the Spirit: Connecting World Church and Local Mission*, (London: Epworth, 2009), 21-22.

[32] Mark Noll, *Turning Points: Decisive Moments in the History of Christianity*, 3rd ed. (Grand Rapids: Baker Academic, 2012), 262.

[33] Andrew Walls, "Afterword: Christian Mission in a Five-hundred-year Context," in *Mission in the 21st Century: Exploring the Five Marks of Global Mission*, eds. Andrew Walls and Cathy Ross (Maryknoll: Orbis Books, 2008), 200.

[34] Noll, *Turning Points*, 264.

[35] Keith Whitfield, "The Triune God: The God of Mission," in *Theology and Practice of Mission: God, the Church, and the Nations*, ed. Bruce R. Ashford (Nashville: B&H Publishing Group, 2011), 18.

[36] Kim, *Joining in with the Spirit*, 23.

[37] Ibid., 32.

[38] Oborji, *Concepts of Mission*, 134.

[39] Kim, *Joining in with the Spirit*, 28.

[40] John Flett, *The Witness of God: The Trinity, Missio Dei, Karl Barth, and the Nature of Christian Community* (Grand Rapids: Wm. B. Eerdmans Publishing Company, 2010), 12.

[41] Oborji, *Concepts of Mission*, 134.

[42] Bevans and Schroeder, *Constants in Context*, 57.

[43] Kemper, "The *Missio Dei* in Contemporary Context," 189.

[44] Oborji, *Concepts of Mission*, 134.

[45] Bosch, *Transforming Mission: Paradigm Shifts*, 2011:379.

[46] Craig Van Gelder and Dwight Zscheile, *The Missional Church in Perspective: Mapping Trends and Shaping Conversations* (Grand Rapids: Baker Academic, 2011), 30.

[47] Oborji, *Concepts of Mission*, 135.

[48] Whitfield, "The Triune God: the God of Mission," 18.

[49] Oborji, *Concepts of Mission*, 135.

[50] Kim, *Joining in with the Spirit*, 25.

[51] J. Andrew Kirk, *What is Mission?* (Minneapolis: Fortress Press, 2000), 24.

[52] Oborji, *Concepts of Mission*, 144.

[53] Ibid.

[54] Van Gelder and Zscheile, *The Missional Church in Perspective*, 30.

[55] Ibid.

[56] Kim, *Joining in with the Spirit*, 26.

[57] Bosch, *Transforming Mission: Paradigm Shifts*, 1991:389.

[58] LCWEa (Lausanne Committee for World Evangelization), *Lausanne Covenant*. Accessed 14 January 2014. http://www.lausanne.org/en/documents/lausanne-covenant.html.

[59] LCWEb *Manila Manifesto*. Accessed 14 January 2014. http://www.lausanne.org/en/documents/manila-manifesto.html.

[60] Scott Sunquist, *Understanding Christian Mission: Participation in Suffering and Glory* (Grand Rapids: Baker Academic, 2013), 159.

[61] LM 2010 (Lausanne Movement), *Cape Town Commitment*. Accessed 14 January 2014. http://www.lausanne.org/en/documents/ctcommitment.html.

[62] Christopher Wright, *The Mission of God: Unlocking the Bible's Grand Narratives* (Downers Grove: IVP Academic, 2006), 67.

[63] Daryl Balia and Kirsteen Kim, eds., *Edinburgh 2010 Volume II: Witnessing to Christ Today* (Oxford: Regnum Books International, 2010), 11, 23.

[64] Kemper, "The *Missio Dei* in Contemporary Context," 189.

[65] Jooseop Keum, ed., *Together Towards Life: Mission and Evangelism in Changing Landscapes, with a Practical Guide* (Geneva: WCC Publications, 2013), 5.

[66] Cathy Ross, "Introduction: Taonga," in *Mission in the 21st Century: Exploring the Five Marks of Global Mission*, eds. Andrew Walls and Cathy Ross (Maryknoll: Orbis Books, 2008), xiv.

[67] Kim, *Joining in with the Spirit*, 29-30.

[68] Emma Wild-Wood and Peniel Rajkumar, *Foundations for Mission* (Oxford: Regnum Books International, 2013), 6-7.

[69] Ibid.

[70] Simangaliso Kumalo, "The Bible in and through Mission and Mission in the Bible in Postcolonial Africa," in *Foundations for Mission*, eds. Emma Wild-Wood and Peniel Rajkumar (Oxford: Regnum Books International, 2013), 97.

[71] Néstor Miguez, "Biblical Foundations for Liberative Mission from Latin America," in *Foundations for Mission*, eds. Emma Wild-Wood and Peniel Rajkumar (Oxford: Regnum Books International, 2013), 94.

[72] John Driver, *Images of the Church in Mission* (Scottsdale, AZ: Herald Press, 1997), 220.

[73] Gary Tyra, *A Missional Orthodoxy: Theology and Ministry in a Post-Christian Context* (Downers Grove: IVP Academic, 2013), 310.

[74] Wild-Wood and Rajkumar, *Foundations for Mission*, 290.

[75] Flett, *The Witness of God*, 76.

[76] Bosch, *Transforming Mission: Paradigm Shifts*, 2011:512.

[77] Stephen Neill, *Creative Tension: The Duff Lectures, 1958* (London: Edinburgh House Press, 1959), 81.

[78] Kirk, *What is Mission?*, 25.

[79] Christopher Wright, *The Mission of God: Unlocking the Bible's Grand Narratives* (Downers Grove: IVP Academic, 2006), 24; Dean Flemming, *Recovering the Full Mission of God: A Biblical Perspective on Being, Doing and Telling* (Downers Grove: IVP Academic, 2013), 18.

[80] Tyra, *A Missional Orthodoxy*, 311.

[81] Darrell Guder, ed., *Missional Church: A Vision for the Sending of the Church in North America* (Grand Rapids: Wm. B. Eerdmans Publishing Company, 1998).

[82] Lois Barrett, "Defining Missional Church," in *Evangelical, Ecumenical and Anabaptist Missiologies in Conversation*, eds. James Krabill, Walter Sawatsky, and Charles Van Engen (Maryknoll: Orbis Books, 2006), 179.

[83] Van Gelder and Zscheile, *The Missional Church in Perspective*, 45.

[84] Charles Van Engen, *God's Missionary People: Rethinking the Purpose of the Local Church* (Grand Rapids: Baker Academic, 1991), 141.

[85] Michael W. Goheen, *A Light to the Nations: The Missional Church and the Biblical Story* (Grand Rapids: Baker Academic, 2011), 4.

[86] Alan Hirsch, *The Forgotten Ways* (Grand Rapids: Brazos Press, 2006), 82.

[87] Barrett, "Defining Missional Church," 177-184.

[88] Tyra, *A Missional Orthodoxy*, 312.

[89] Bosch, *Transforming Mission: Paradigm Shifts*, 2011:281.

[90] Lois Barrett, *Treasures in Clay Jars: Patterns in Missional Faithfulness* (Grand Rapids: Wm. B. Eerdmans Publishing Company, 2004), 140.

[91] Roxburgh, *The Missional Leader*, 5.

[92] Van Gelder and Zscheile, *The Missional Church in Perspective*, 156.

[93] Ibid., 155.

[94] Barrett, *Treasures in Clay Jars*, 140.

[95] Roxburgh and Romanuk, *The Missional Leader*, 5.

[96] Van Gelder and Zscheile, *The Missional Church in Perspective*, 156.

[97] C. J. P. (Nelus) Niemandt, *Nuwe leiers vir nuwe werklikhede* (Vereeniging: CUM, 2013), 57.

[98] Bosch, *Transforming Mission: Paradigm Shifts*, 2011:500-501.

## Chapter 2: Globalization and Glocalization in the *Missio Dei*

[1] Anthony Giddens, *The Third Way* (Cambridge: Polity Press, 1998), 64.

[2] Richard Tiplady, ed., *One World or Many? The Impact of Globalization on Mission* (Pasadena: William Carey Library, 2003), 2.

[3] Stephen Roach, *Stephen Roach on the Next Asia: Opportunities and Challenges for a New Globalization* (Hoboken: John Wiley & Sons, 2009), 89.

[4] Maria Livanos Cattaui, "Opportunities in the Global Economy," in *Community of the Future*, eds. Frances Hesselbein, Marshall Goldsmith, Richard Beckhard, and Richard F. Schubert (New York: Jossey-Bass, 1998), 168.

[5] Manfred Steger, *Globalization: A Very Short Introduction* (New York: Oxford University Press, 2003), 13.

[6] Jehu Hanciles, *Beyond Christendom: Globalization, African Migration, and the Transformation of the West* (Maryknoll: Orbis Books, 2008), 15.

[7] Nayef R. F. Al-Rodhan, *Definitions of Globalization: A Comprehensive Overview and a Proposed Definition* (Geneva: Geneva Centre for Security Policy, 2006), 5.

[8] James H. Mittelman, *The Globalization Syndrome: Transformation and Resistance* (Princeton: Princeton University Press, 2000), 7.

[9] Manuel Castells, *The Power of Identity*, 2nd ed. (West Sussex: Wiley-Blackwell, 2010), 304.

[10] Thomas L. Friedman, *The World is Flat: a Brief History of the 21st Century* (New York: Farrar, Straus and Giroux, 2005), 9.

[11] Ibid.

[12] Castells, *The Power of Identity*, xxxiv.

[13] Hanciles, *Beyond Christendom*, 23.

[14] WCC (World Council of Churches), *Resource book*, World Council of Churches, 10th Assembly Busan (Geneva: WCC Publications, 2013), 181.

[15] Hanciles, *Beyond Christendom*, 204.

[16] Jan A. Scholte, *Globalization: A Critical Introduction*, (London: Macmillan, 2000), 45.

[17] Ibid., 207.

[18] Hanciles, *Beyond Christendom*, 72.

[19] Peter Berger, "Four Faces of Global Culture," in *Globalization and the Challenges of a New Century*, eds. Patrick O'Meara, Howard D. Mehlinger, and Matthew Krain (Indianapolis: Indiana University Press, 2000), 427.

[20] Roach, *Stephen Roach on the Next Asia*, 128.

[21] Ibid., 89.

[22] Ibid., 11.

[23] Patrick Dixon, "Global Trends, People Movements, and Their Impact on Mission," in *Lausanne Global Analysis*, June, 2013:9.

[24] Mac Pier, "Global City Influence: A Personal Reflection," in *Lausanne Global Analysis*, June, 2013:21.

[25] Ibid.

[26] James Hunter, *To Change the World: The Irony, Tragedy, and Possibility of Christianity in the Late Modern World* (New York: Oxford University Press, 2011), 200.

[27] Mittelman, *The Globalization Syndrome*, 4.

[28] Hanciles, *Beyond Christendom*, 28.

[29] Michael W. Goheen, *A Light to the Nations: The Missional Church and the Biblical Story* (Grand Rapids: Baker Academic, 2011), 14.

[30] Ibid.

[31] Anthony Giddens, *Runaway World: How Globalization is Reshaping Our Lives* (New York: Rutledge, 2003), 13.

[32] Castells, *The Power of Identity*, 304.

[33] Ronald Aronica and Mtetwa Ramdoo, *The World is Flat?* (Tampa: Meghan-Kifter Press, 2006), 17.

[34] Goheen, *A Light to the Nations*, 14.

[35] David Smith, *Mission After Christendom* (London: Darton, Longman & Todd, 2003), 94.

[36] Richard Gaillardetz, *The Church in the Making: Lumen Gentium, Christus Dominus, Orientalium Ecclesiarum* (Mahwah: Paulist Press, 2006), 158.

[37] Giddens, *Runaway World*, 13.

[38] Harold Netland, "Introduction: Globalization and Theology Today," in *Globalizing Theology: Belief and Practice in an Era of World Christianity*, eds. Craig Ott and Harold Netland (Grand Rapids: Baker Academic, 2006), 19.

[39] Philip Jenkins, *The Next Christendom: The Coming of Global Christianity*, 3rd ed. (New York: Oxford University Press, 2011), xi.

[40] Robert Wuthnow, *Boundless Faith: The Global Outreach of American Churches* (Berkley: University of California Press, 2009), 74.

[41] Ibid., 45.

[42] Berger, "Four Faces of Global Culture," 425.

[43] Hanciles, *Beyond Christendom*, 52.

[44] Berger, "Four Faces of Global Culture," 427.

[45] Netland, "Globalization and Theology Today," 24.

[46] Wuthnow, *Boundless Faith*, 65.

[47] Hanciles, *Beyond Christendom*, 127.

[48] S. Hun Kim, "Migrant Workers and 'Reverse Mission' in the West," in *Korean Diaspora and Christian Mission*, eds. H.S. Kim and Wonsuk Ma (Oxford: Regnum Books International, 2011), 147.

[49] Dana Robert, *Christian Mission: How Christianity Became a World Religion* (Chichester: John Wiley & Sons, 2009), 73.

[50] Ibid.

[51] Wuthnow, *Boundless Faith*, 91.

[52] Samuel Escobar, "Mission from Everywhere to Everyone: The Home Base in a New Century," in *Edinburgh 2010: Mission Then and Now*, eds. David A. Kerr and Kenneth R. Ross (Oxford: Regnum Books International, 2009), 195.

[53] Hanciles, *Beyond Christendom*, 36.

[54] Kevin Vanhoozer, "One Rule to Rule Them All?," in *Globalizing Theology: Belief and Practice in an Era of World Christianity*, eds. Craig Ott and Harold Netland (Grand Rapids: Baker Academic, 2006), 99.

[55] Roland Robertson, *Globalization: Social Theory and Global Culture* (London: SAGE, 1992), 172-173.

[56] Wuthnow, *Boundless Faith*, 77.

[57] Charles E. Van Engen, "The Glocal Church: Locality and Catholicity in a Globalizing World," in *Globalizing Theology: Belief and Practice in an Era of World Christianity*, eds. Craig Ott and Harold A. Netland (Grand Rapids: Baker Academic, 2006), 159.

[58] Fareed Zakaria, *The Post-American World and the Rise of the Rest* (London: Penguin, 2009), 82.

[59] Hanciles, *Beyond Christendom*, 61.

[60] Wuthnow, *Boundless Faith*, 77.

[61] Lamin Sanneh, *Translating the Message: The Missionary Impact on Culture* (Maryknoll: Orbis Books, 1989), 51.

[62] Kwame Bediako, *Jesus and the Gospel in Africa: History and Experience* (Maryknoll: Orbis Books, 2004), 32.

[63] Lamin Sanneh, *Whose Religion is Christianity? The Gospel Beyond the West* (Grand Rapids: Wm. B. Eerdmans Publishing Company, 2003), 97.

[64] Jenkins, *The Next Christendom*, 217.

[65] Ibid.

[66] Manuel Castells, Mireia Fernández-Ardèvol, Jack Linchuan Qiu and Araba Sey, *Mobile Communication and Society: A Global Perspective* (Cambridge: MIT Press, 2007), 174.

[67] Bryan S. Turner, *Religion and Modern Society: Citizenship, Secularization, and the State* (Cambridge: Cambridge University Press, 2011), 247.

[68] Roland Robertson, "Glocalization: Time-Space and Homogeneity-Heterogeneity," in *Global Modernities*, eds. Mike Featherstone, Scott Lash, and Roland Robertson (London: SAGE, 1995), 28.

[69] Van Engen, "The Glocal Church," 157.

[70] Robertson, *Social Theory and Global Culture*, 173.

## Chapter 3: Paradigm Shifts and Polycentrism in the *Missio Dei*

[1] Thomas Kuhn, *The Structure of Scientific Revolutions*, 50th anniversary ed. (Chicago: University of Chicago Press, 2012), 23.

[2] Rory McDowall Clark and Janet Murray, *Reconceptualizing Leadership in the Early Years* (Maidenhead: Open University Press, 2012), 4.

[3] Kuhn, *Scientific Revolutions*, 150.

[4] David Bosch, *Transforming Mission: Paradigm Shifts in Theology of Mission*, 20th anniversary ed. (Maryknoll: Orbis Books, 2011), 189.

[5] Anne Wilson Schaef and Diane Fassel, *The Addictive Organization* (New York: HarperOne, 1988), 34.

[6] Kuhn, *Scientific Revolutions*, xxviii.

[7] Ibid., 157.

[8] Ibid., 155.

[9] Ibid., 168.

[10] Hans Küng, *Theology for the Third Millennium* (New York: Anchor Books, 1988), 144.

[11] Schaef and Fassel, *The Addictive Organization*, 25.

[12] Kuhn, *Scientific Revolutions*, 9.

[13] Küng, *Theology for the Third Millennium*, 128-152.

[14] Ibid., 128.

[15] Fernando Canale, "Paradigm, System and Theological Pluralism," *Evangelical Quarterly* 70, 195-218, 1998:202.

[16] Bosch, *Transforming Mission*, 2011:192.

[17] Ibid., 1.

[18] Ibid., 192.

[19] Ibid.

[20] Dictionary.com, s.v. polycentrism, *Dictionary.com Unabridged*. Random House, Inc. http://www.dictionary.com/browse/polycentrism (accessed: 2015).

[21] David Ahstrom and Garry D. Bruton, *International Management: Strategy and Culture in the Emerging World* (Mason: South-Western Cengage Learning, 2010), 42.

[22] Ibid.

[23] Daryl Balia and Kirsteen Kim, eds., *Edinburgh 2010 volume II: Witnessing to Christ Today* (Oxford: Regnum Books International, 2010), 255.

[24] Michael Byram, Adam Nichols, and David Stevens, eds., *Developing Intercultural Competence in Practice* (Clevendon: Multilingual Matters Ltd, 2001), 5.

[25] Ibid.

[26] Gary L. Bowen, James A. Martin, Jay A. Mancini, and John P. Nelson, *Community Capacity: Antecedents and Consequences*, n.d., ca 2000, viewed 15 March 2014, from http://www.fcs.uga.edu/cfd/fcrlweb/docs/ccb/2000_Bowen_Martin_Mancini_Nelson.pdf.

[27] Ron Hustedde, "What's Culture Got to do With It? Strategies for Strengthening Entrepreneurial Culture," in *Entrepreneurship and Local Economic Development*, ed. Norman Walzer (Plymouth: Lexington Books, 2007), 53.

[28] Ori Brafman and Rod A. Beckstrom, *The Starfish and the Spider* (New York: Penguin, 2006), 19.

[29] Ibid., 46.

[30] Ibid., 50.

[31] Ibid.

[32] Ibid., 35.

[33] Ibid., 87.

[34] Ibid., 95, 206.

[35] Ibid., 89.

[36] Suzanne W. Morse, "Five Building Blocks for Successful Leadership," in *The Community of the Future*, eds. Frances Hesselbein, Marshall Goldsmith, Richard Beckhard, and Richard F. Schubert (San Francisco: Jose Bass, 1998), 234.

[37] Brafman and Beckstrom, *The Starfish and the Spider*, 164.

[38] JR Woodward, *Creating a Missional Culture: Equipping the Church for the Sake of the World* (Downers Grove: InterVarsity Press, 2012), 20.

[39] Ibid., 61.

[40] Ibid., 60.

[41] Ibid., 100.

[42] Ibid., 93.

[43] Balia and Kim, *Witnessing to Christ Today*, 166.

[44] Klaus Koschorke, "Polycentric Structures in the History of World Christianity," in *Polycentric Structures in the History of World Christianity*, eds. Klaus Koschorke and Adrian Hermann (Wiesbaden: Harrassowitz GmbH & Co., 2014), 18.

[45] Ibid.

[46] Ibid., 19.

[47] Tite Tiénou, "Christian Theology in an Era of World Christianity," in *Globalizing Theology: Belief and Practice in an Era of World Christianity*, eds. Craig Ott and Harold Netland (Grand Rapids: Baker Academic, 2006), 38.

[48] Lamin Sanneh, *Translating the Message: The Missionary Impact on Culture* (Maryknoll: Orbis Books, 1989), 51.

[49] Lamin Sanneh, *Whose Religion is Christianity? The Gospel Beyond the West* (Grand Rapids: Wm. B. Eerdmans Publishing Company, 2003), 97.

## Chapter 4: Friendship and Community in the *Missio Dei*

[1] Nancy E. Bedford, "'Speak, "Friend," and Enter': Friendship and Theological Method," in *God's Life in Trinity*, eds. Miroslav Volf and Michael Welker (Minneapolis: Fortress Press, 2006), 35.

2 Ibid.

3 Ibid., 36.

4 How Chuang Chua, "Perichoresis and *Missio Dei*: Implications of a Trinitarian View of Personhood for Missionary Practice," (paper presented at OMF Mission Research Consultation, 2010), 5.

5 Arthur F. Glasser, Charles E. Van Engen, Dean S. Gilliland, and Shawn B. Redford, *Announcing the Kingdom: The Story of God's Mission in the Bible* (Grand Rapids: Baker Academic, 2003), 369.

6 Dana L. Robert, "Cross-cultural Friendship in the Creation of Twentieth-century World Christianity," *International Bulletin of Missionary Research*, 35(2), (April 2011), 106.

7 Jooseop Keum, ed., *Together Towards Life: Mission and Evangelism in Changing Landscapes, with a Practical Guide* (Geneva: WCC Publications, 2013), 35.

8 Daryl Balia and Kirsteen Kim, eds., *Edinburgh 2010 volume II: Witnessing to Christ Today* (Oxford: Regnum Books International, 2010), 47.

9 Kirsteen Kim, *Joining in with the Spirit: Connecting World Church and Local Mission* (London: Epworth, 2009), 23.

10 Robert, "Cross-cultural Friendship," 100.

11 Balia and Kim, *Witnessing to Christ Today*, 133.

12 Brian Stanley, *The World Missionary Conference, Edinburgh 1910* (Grand Rapids: Wm. B. Eerdmans Publishing Company, 2009), 129-130.

13 Robert, "Cross-cultural Friendship," 100.

14 Jonathan Bonk, "Edinburgh 1910: Friendship and the Boundaries of Christendom," *International Bulletin of Missionary Research*, 30 (4), 169-170, 2006a:170.

15 Stanley, *World Missionary Conference*, 130.

16 Robert, "Cross-cultural Friendship," 102.

[17] Ibid., 106.

[18] Ibid., 102.

[19] Janice Price, *World-shaped Mission: Exploring New Frameworks for the Church of England in World Mission* (London: Church House Publishing, 2012), 59.

[20] Robert, "Cross-cultural Friendship," 106.

[21] Dictionary.com, s.v. community, *Dictionary.com Unabridged*. Random House, Inc. http://www.dictionary.com/browse/community (accessed: 2015).

[22] Frances Hesselbein, Marshall Goldsmith, Richard Beckhard, and Richard F. Schubert, eds., *The Community of the Future* (San Francisco: Jossey-Bass, 1998), xi.

[23] WGA, 2014, *The Wycliffe Global Alliance in Community: Principles of Community*, viewed 10 October 2014, from http://www.wycliffe.net/aboutus/positionstatements/tabid/86/Default.aspx?id=5084.

[24] Todd M. Johnson and Cindy M. Wu, *Our Global Families: Christians Embracing Common Identity in a Changing World* (Grand Rapids: Baker Academic, 2015), 140.

[25] Roger Helland and Leonard Hjalmarson, *Missional Spirituality: Embodying God's Love from the Inside Out* (Downers Grove: IVP Books, 2011), 54.

[26] Jedediah Coppenger, "The Community of Mission: the Church," in *Theology and Practice of Mission: God, the Church and the Nations*, ed. Bruce Ashford (Nashville: B&H Publishing Group, 2011), 61.

[27] Charles Van Engen, *God's Missionary People: Rethinking the Purpose of the Local Church* (Grand Rapids: Baker Academic, 1991), 124.

[28] Coppenger "The Community of Mission", 61.

[29] Ibid.

[30] Johnson and Wu, *Our Global Families*, 140.

## Chapter 5: Reflective Practitioners and the Consultative Process in the *Missio Dei*

[1] Kirk Franklin, "A Model for Leadership Communities in Global Contexts," in *The End of Leadership? Leadership and Authority at Crossroads*, vol. 4, Christian Perspectives on Leadership and Social Ethics, eds. Jack Barentsen, Steven C. van den Heuvel, and Peirong Lin (Leuven: Peeters, 2017), 105.

[2] Deenabandhu Manchala, Peniel Rajkumar, and Dayam Joseph Prabhakar, "When Margins Inform and Re-form Mission," in *Foundations for Mission*, eds. Emma Wild-Wood and Peniel Rajkumar (Oxford: Regnum Books International, 2013), 32.

[3] William Taylor, ed., *Global Missiology for the 21st Century: The Iguassu Dialogue* (Grand Rapids: Baker Academic, 2000), 1.

[4] Ibid., 550; Franklin, "A Model for Leadership Communities," 103.

[5] Susan Van Wynen, "Looking to Jesus: Lessons in Becoming a Reflective Practitioner" (unpublished paper, 2008).; Franklin, "A Model for Leadership Communities," 104.

[6] David Rock, *Quiet leadership* (New York: HarperCollins, 2006) e-book.

[7] Eddie Gibbs, *Leadershipnext: Changing Leaders in a Changing Culture* (Downers Grove: InterVarsity, 2005), 136.

[8] Roger Helland and Leonard Hjalmarson, *Missional Spirituality: Embodying God's Love from the Inside Out* (Downers Grove: IVP Books, 2011), 49.

[9] Mark Sayers, *Facing Leviathan: Leadership, Influence, and Creating in a Cultural Storm* (Chicago: Moody Publishers, 2014:126.; Franklin "A Model for Leadership Communities," 104-5.

[10] REC (Reformed Ecumenical Council), "Clerical and Lay Leadership" (unpublished paper, 2005).; Franklin, "A Model for Leadership Communities," 104.

[11] Alan Roxburgh and Fred Romanuk, *The Missional Leader: Equipping Your Church to Reach a Changing World* (San Francisco: Josey-Bass, 2006), 176.

[12] Stephen Coertze, *What is a Missiological Consultation?* (unpublished paper, 2013a:1).

[13] Ibid.

[14] Ibid.

[15] Ibid.

## Chapter 6: Generosity in Spirit and Practice in the *Missio Dei*

[1] *Merriam-Webster Dictionary*, 2016, s.vv. "coin of the realm."

[2] Scott Sunquist, *Understanding Christian Mission: Participation in Suffering and Glory* (Grand Rapids: Baker Academic, 2013), 381.

[3] Alex Araujo and Werner Mischke, "A Report on 'Catching the Wind—A Sailing Retreat': Contrasting the 'Powerboat' and 'Sailboat' Mindset for Leadership," (unpublished document, 2009), 2.

[4] Eckbald Schnabel, *Paul the Missionary: Realities, Strategies and Methods* (Downers Grove: IVP Academic, 2008), 442-3.

[5] Ibid., 444.

[6] Gilles Gravelle, *The Age of Global Giving: A Practical Guide for Donors and Funding Recipients of Our Time* (Pasadena:William Carey Library, 2014), Kindle Edition, loc 882.

[7] Ibid., 1000.

[8] Ibid., 579.

[9] Ibid., 1121.

[10] McGlory T. Speckman, *A Biblical Vision for Africa's Development* (Pietermartizburg: Cluster Publications, 2007), 250.

[11] Jonathan Bonk, *Missions and Money*, revised and expanded (Maryknoll: Orbis Books, 2006b), 156.

[12] Kelly M. Kapic, *God So Loved, He Gave* (Grand Rapids: Zondervan, 2010), 10.

[13] R. Scott Rodin, "A Vision for the Generous Life," in *Christ-centered Generosity: Global Perspectives on the Biblical Call to a Generous Life*, ed. R. Scott Rodin (Colbert: Kingdom Life Publishers, 2015), 11.

[14] Dennis Tongoi, "Living Generously in an African Culture," in *Christ-centered Generosity: Global Perspectives on the Biblical Call to a Generous Life*, ed. R. Scott Rodin (Colbert: Kingdom Life Publishers, 2015), 66.

[15] Kapic, *God So Loved*, 10.

[16] Tongoi, "Living Generously," 65.

[17] Zenet Maramara, "Biblical Stewardship: The Foundation of All Generosity," in *Christ-centered Generosity: Global Perspectives on the Biblical Call to a Generous Life*, ed. R. Scott Rodin (Colbert: Kingdom Life Publishers, 2015), 141.

[18] Kapic, *God So Loved*, 192.

[19] Robert Reese, *Roots and Remedies: Of the Dependency Syndrome in World Missions* (Pasadena: William Carey Library, 2010), 89.

[20] Ibid.

[21] Bonk, *Missions and Money*, 2006b:156.

[22] Ibid.

[23] Miroslav Volf, "Being as God Is: Trinity and Generosity," in *God's Life in Trinity*, eds. Miroslav Volf and Michael Welker (Minneapolis: Fortress Press, 2006), 8.

[24] Stephen Coertze, "Funding God's Mission: Exploring a Missiological Response to Undergird Future Practice," (Global Funding Consultation report for Wycliffe Global Alliance, unpublished paper, Antalya, Turkey, September 2013b).

[25] Ibid.

[26] Minyoung Jung, "Global Funding Consultation," (report for Wycliffe Global Alliance, Antalya, Turkey, September 2013).

[27] Kirk Franklin, "Wycliffe Global Alliance Principles for Funding in the Context of God's Mission," (unpublished paper, 2014), 1.

## Chapter 7: Third Way Thinking in the *Missio Dei*

[1] Andrew Walls, "Demographics, Power and the Gospel in the 21st Century," (paper presented at the Wycliffe International Convention and the SIL International Conference, Waxhaw, 2002), 1.

[2] Ibid.

[3] Mary Uhl-Bien, Russ Marion, and Bill McKelvey, 2007, "Complexity Leadership Theory: Shifting Leadership from the Industrial Age to the Knowledge Era," *The Leadership Quarterly*, 18, 298-318, doi:10.1016/j. leaqua.2007.04.002.

[4] Thomas L. Saaty, 2014, "The Three Laws of Thought, Plus One: The Law of Comparisons," in *Axioms*, 3(1), 46-49, doi:10.3390/axioms3010046.

[5] Richard E. Nisbett *et al.*, in Brian Huss, 2004:376, "Cultural Differences and the Law of Noncontradiction: Some Criteria for Further Research," *Philosophical Psychology*, 17(3), 375-389, DOI: 10.1080/0951508042000286730.

[6] Brian Huss, 2004:375, "Cultural Differences and the Law of Noncontradiction: Some Criteria for Further Research," *Philosophical Psychology*, 17(3), 375-389, DOI: 10.1080/0951508042000286730.

[7] Dictionary.com, s.v. binary, *Dictionary.com Unabridged*. Random House, Inc. http://www.dictionary.com/browse/binary (accessed: 2016).

[8] Charles Van Engen, *Mission on the Way: Issues in Mission Theology* (Grand Rapids: Baker Books, 1996), 26.

[9] Ray Oldenburg, *The Great Good Place: Cafés, Coffee Shops, Bookstores, Bars, Hair Salons, and Other Hangouts at the Heart of a Community* (Cambridge: Da Capo Press, 1999).

[10] Matthew Carmona, Steve Tiesdell, Tim Heath, and Taner Oc, *Public Places, Urban Spaces: The Dimensions of Urban Design*, 2nd ed. (Oxford: Architectural Press, 2010), 139.

[11] Oldenburg, *The Great Good Place*, 33.

[12] Constance A. Steinkuehler and Dmitri Williams, 2006:885, "Where Everybody Knows Your (Screen) Name: Online Games as 'Third Places,'" in *Journal of Computer-Mediated Communication*, 11(4), 885-909, doi:10.1111/j.1083-6101.2006.00300.x.

[13] Jeanne Stevenson-Moessner, *Portable Roots: Transplanting the Bicultural Child* (Newcastle upon Tyneui: Cambridge Scholars Publishing, 2014), 23.

[14] David C. Pollock and Ruth E. Van Reken, *Third Culture Kids: Growing Up Among Worlds*, rev. ed. (Boston: Nichols Brealey Publishing, 2009), 13.

[15] Stevenson-Moessner, *Portable Roots*, 26.

[16] Pollock and Van Reken, *Third Culture Kids*, 13.

[17] Ibid., 14-15.

[18] Ibid., 17.

[19] Adam Fraser, *The Third Space: Using Life's Little Transitions to Find Balance and Happiness* (North Sydney: Random House, 2012), 9.

[20] Ibid., 10.

[21] Jonathan Rutherford, "The Third Space: Interview with Homi Bhabha," in *Identity: Community, Culture , Difference* (London: Lawrence and Wishart, 1990), 207-221.

[22] Janice Price, *World-shaped Mission: Exploring New Frameworks for the Church of England in World Mission* (London: Church House Publishing, 2012), 59.

[23] Christopher R. Baker, *The Hybrid Church in the City* (Aldershot: Ashgate Publishing, 2007), 68.

[24] Ibid.

[25] Ibid., 24.

[26] Ibid., 68.

[27] Ibid., 106.

[28] Ibid.

[29] Ibid., 111.

[30] Dorothy Stroh Becvar and Raphael J. Becvar, *Family Therapy: A Systemic Integration* (Essex: Pearson Education, 2014).

[31] Stephen Coertze, "Third Spaces and Reflective Processes in the Context of Systems Theory" (unpublished paper of May, 2016).

## Chapter 8: Forming a Global Missional Mindset

[1] Robert P. Vecchio, ed., *Leadership: Understanding the Dynamics of Power and Influence in Organizations* (Notre Dame: University of Notre Dame Press, 1997), 320.

[2] Vecchio, *Understanding the Dynamics of Power*, 431.

[3] Timothy Laniak, *Shepherds After My Own Heart: Pastoral Traditions and Leadership in the Bible* (Downers Grove: InterVarsity Press, 2006), 247.

[4] REC (Reformed Ecumenical Council), "Clerical and Lay Leadership" (unpublished paper, 2005), 69.

[5] Martin Chemers, *An Integrative Theory of Leadership* (Mahwah: Lawrence Erlbaum, 1997), 119.

[6] Robert J. Banks and Bernice M. Ledbetter, *Reviewing Leadership: A Christian Evaluation of Current Approaches* (Grand Rapids: Baker Academic, 2004).

[7] Allen J. Morrison, "Developing a Global Leadership Model," *Human Resource Management* 39(2-3), 117-131. (2000:118).

[8] Morrison, "Global Leadership Model," 119.

[9] Ibid.

[10] Ernest Gundling, Terry Hogan, and Karen Cvitkovich, *What is Global Leadership?* (London: Nicholas Brealey Publishing, 2011), 15.

[11] Ibid.

[12] Mark E. Mendenhall et al., *Global Leadership: Research, Practice and Development*, 2nd ed. (New York: Routledge, 2013), 17.

[13] Morrison, "Global Leadership Model," 120.

[14] Chris Start and Peirong Lin, "The Search for Spirituality in the Business World," in *Leadership, Innovation and Spirituality*, eds. Patrick Nullens and Jack Barentsen (Leuven: Peeters, 2014), 37.

[15] Larry Richards, *A Practical Theology of Spirituality* (Grand Rapids: Academie/Zondervan, 1987), 49.

[16] Dallas Willard, *Hearing God: Developing a Conversational Relationship with God*, updated and expanded by Jan Johnson (Downers Grove: IVP Books, 2012), 288.

[17] Ruth Haley Barton, *Pursuing God's Will Together* (Downers Grove: InterVarsity Press, 2012), 64.

[18] Robert E. Webber, *The Younger Evangelicals* (Grand Rapids: Baker Books, 2002), 240.

[19] Scott Sunquist, *Understanding Christian Mission: Participation in Suffering and Glory* (Grand Rapids: Baker Academic, 2013), 399ff.

[20] Anne-Marie Kool, "Changing Images in the Formation for Mission: Commission Five in Light of Current Challenges: A Western Perspective," in *Edinburgh 2010: Mission Then and Now*, eds. David A. Kerr and Kenneth R. Ross (Pasadena: William Carey International Press, 2009), 159-160.

[21] Samuel Kobia, "Cooperation and the Promotion of Unity: A World Council of Churches Perspective," in *Edinburgh 2010: mission then and now*, eds. David A. Kerr and Kenneth R. Ross (Pasadena: William Carey International Press, 2009), 246.

[22] David Bosch, *Transforming Mission: Paradigm Shifts in Theology of Mission*, 20th anniversary ed. (Maryknoll: Orbis Books, 2011), 238.

[23] Patrick G. Henry, "Monastic Mission: The Monastic Tradition as Source for Unity and Renewal Today," *Ecumenical Review* XXXIX(3), (1987:280) 271-281.

[24] Jooseop Keum, ed., *Together Towards Life: Mission and Evangelism in Changing Landscapes, with a Practical Guide* (Geneva: WCC Publications, 2013), 38.

[25] Moises Naim, *The End of Power: From Boardrooms to Battlefields and Churches to States, Why Being in Charge Isn't What It Used to Be* (New York: Basic Books, 2013), Kindle, 16.

[26] Hans J. Morgenthau, *Politics in the Twentieth Century: The Impasse of American Foreign Policy* (Chicago: University of Chicago Press, 1962), 141.

[27] Simon Reich and Richard N. Lebow, *Good-bye Hegemony! Power and Influence in the Global System* (Princeton: Princeton University Press, 2014), 28.

[28] Ronald A. Heifetz, Alexander Grashow, and Marty Linsky, *The Practice of Adaptive Leadership: Tools and Tactics for Changing Your Organization and the World* (Boston: Harvard Business School Publishing, 2009), 24.

[29] Barbara Kellerman, *The End of Leadership* (New York: Harper Collins, 2012), 39.

[30] Moises, *The End of Power*, loc 288.

[31] Kellerman, *The End of Leadership*, 46.

[32] Ibid., 49.

[33] Ibid., 54.

[34] Jon Tyson, foreword to *Facing Leviathan: Leadership, Influence, and Creating in a Cultural Storm*, by Mark Sayers (Chicago: Moody Publishers, Chicago, 2014), 7-8.

[35] Anne Schaef and Diane Fassel, *The Addictive Organization* (New York: HarperOne, 1988), 80.

[36] Sayers, *Facing Leviathan*, 114.

[37] Schaef and Fassel, *The Addictive Organization*, 135.

[38] Kellerman, *The End of Leadership*, 69.

[39] Moises, *The End of Power*, 1.

[40] Kellerman, *The End of Leadership*, 72.

[41] Moises, *The End of Power*, 510.

[42] Ibid., 230.

[43] Ibid., 236.

[44] Kellerman, *The End of Leadership*, 96.

[45] Ibid., 169.

[46] Ibid.

[47] Kellerman, *The End of Leadership*, 179.

[48] Sayers, *Facing Leviathan*, 217.

[49] Michael W. Goheen, *A Light to the Nations: The Missional Church and the Biblical Story* (Grand Rapids: Baker Academic, 2011), 4.

[50] Charles E. Van Engen, *God's Missionary People: Rethinking the Purpose of the Local Church* (Grand Rapids: Baker Academic, 1991), 141.

[51] Craig Van Gelder and Dwight J. Zscheile, *The Missional Church in Perspective: Mapping Trends and Shaping Conversations* (Grand Rapids: Baker Academic, 2011), 156.

52 C. J. P. (Nelus) Niemandt, "Missional Leadership—Entering the Trialogue" (inaugural address as head of the Department of Science of Religion and Missiology, University of Pretoria, South Africa, 2012), 9-12.

53 Philip R. Harris, Robert T. Moran, and Sarah V. Moran, *Managing Cultural Differences: Global Leadership Strategies for the Twenty-first Century*, 6th ed. (Burlington: Elsevier Butterworth-Heinemann, 2004), 25.

54 Gundling et al., *What is Global Leadership?*, 29-30, 36, 54, 75, 95, 186, 188.

55 Mary Uhl-Bien, Russ Marion, and Bill McKelvey, "Complexity Leadership Theory: Shifting Leadership from the Industrial Age to the Knowledge Era." *The Leadership Quarterly*, 18, no. 4 (2007:299): 298-318, doi:10.1016/j.leaqua.2007.04.002.

56 Ibid., 302.

57 Ibid., 301.

58 Sayers, *Facing Leviathan*, 70.

59 Ibid., 194.

60 Leonard Sweet, *I Am a Follower: The Way, Truth, and Life of Following Jesus* (Nashville: Thomas Nelson, 2012), 12.

61 Anne Schaef and Diane Fassel, *The Addictive Organization* (New York: HarperOne, 1988), 226.

62 Sayers, *Facing Leviathan*, 131.

63 Ibid., 125.

64 Kirk Franklin, "A Model for Leadership Communities in Global Contexts," in *The End of Leadership? Leadership and Authority at Crossroads*, vol. 4, Christian Perspectives on Leadership and Social Ethics, eds. Jack Barentsen, Steven C. van den Heuvel, and Peirong Lin (Leuven: Peeters, 2017), 90-91.

# ABOUT THE AUTHOR

## Kirk J. Franklin

Serving in God's mission has always been part of Kirk's life. He is a missionary kid born in Papua New Guinea (PNG), where he grew up amongst the Kewa people. Kirk joined Wycliffe US in 1980 as a media-communications specialist and served with SIL International, and the PNG Bible Translation Association.

His academic qualifications are a BA in Intercultural Studies, Tabor College Victoria; BA (Honors) (Theology), MA (Theology), and PhD from the University of Pretoria, South Africa, where his research focused on a paradigm for global mission leadership.

Since 2008, Kirk has been the Executive Director of the Wycliffe Global Alliance (WGA)—comprised of 100 organizations. Prior to this, he held leadership roles in Wycliffe Australia for 16 years. Kirk is often called upon to speak at conferences and events around the world—a chief topic being his vision for leaders in God's mission to develop a global missional mindset so they have a greater understanding and capacity to lead well and responsibly in the constantly changing contexts in which they serve.

Kirk is married to Christine, and they have three adult children and two grandsons. The Franklins live in Melbourne, Australia and are active members of Warrandyte Community Church.

To contact Dr Franklin: kirkfranklin31@gmail.com

· · ·

### Book collaborators and co-editors, Dave and Deborah Crough

Dave and Deborah have served with Wycliffe Bible Translators since 1984. They have lived in Papua New Guinea, France, Cameroon and Canada, where they raised their two (now adult) children. They each hold a BA in Communication Arts from Loyola Marymount University, Los Angeles, and Dave holds an MS in Photography from Brooks Institute of Photography. Both have worked in various aspects of media production, including photography, feature article writing and editorial roles. In 2007, they produced a book published by Wycliffe Canada entitled, *Eye to Eye, Heart to Heart*. Deborah is a communications consultant with WGA, and Dave is a special projects consultant on the WGA leadership team. They reside in California.